CW01622069

Edward M. Barringer

Ancient Collects

AND OTHER PRAYERS,

SELECTED FOR DEVOTIONAL USE
FROM VARIOUS RITUALS,

WITH

An Appendix, on the Collects in the Prayer-Book.

BY

WILLIAM BRIGHT, M.A.,
FELLOW OF UNIVERSITY COLLEGE, OXFORD;
AUTHOR OF "A HISTORY OF THE CHURCH FROM A.D. 313 TO A.D. 451."

Second Edition, Enlarged.

Oxford & London:
J. H. AND JAS. PARKER.
1862.

~~III-970~~
C 9930.2.17 1881, April 8.
Barringer's bequest.

HARVARD UNIVERSITY LIBRARY

"AND THOU CONTINUEST HOLY: O THOU WORSHIP OF ISRAEL.

"OUR FATHERS HOPED IN THEE: THEY TRUSTED IN THEE, AND THOU DIDST DELIVER THEM.

"THEY CALLED UPON THEE, AND WERE HOLPEN; THEY PUT THEIR TRUST IN THEE, AND WERE NOT CONFOUNDED."

1521
54-135
32

TO THE REVEREND

DANIEL FOX SANDFORD,

SENIOR CURATE OF S. JOHN THE EVANGELIST'S,

AND CHAPLAIN TO THE HOUSE OF MERCY, EDINBURGH,

This Manual

IS MOST AFFECTIONATELY INSCRIBED.

PREFACE.

THE following pages are designed to contribute somewhat to a more practical knowledge among Churchmen of the devotional treasures to be found in ancient Service-books. They contain, it need not be said, the merest gatherings from an ample and splendid storehouse,—a few drops from a cup filled to overflowing.

The majority of the Prayers here translated are taken from Western rituals older than Anglo-Saxon Christianity; especially from those Sacramentaries of Leo the Great, Gelasius the First, and Gregory the Great, which still supply the English Church with so many inestimable Collects, and would probably have been made still more serviceable at the last revision of the Prayer-Book, had they all been then accessible [a]. Many of the

[a] A Sacramentary consisted of three elements: 1. the principal and invariable portions of the Liturgy or Mass; 2. all the varying *proper* prayers, as collects, secrets, post-communions, and the like; 3. some other ritual forms. It was also called the Book of Mysteries, the Book of Sacraments, eventually the Missal. The Gelasian and Leonine Sacramentaries were not edited when our Prayer-Book was settled in 1661. Some account of the three great Roman Sacramentaries will be found in the Appendix.

Collects now presented to the reader seem quite equal in depth and beauty to those well-known specimens of their class which the child's ear so readily welcomes, and the man's heart finds so inexhaustible.

Other Western Prayers have been admitted, of later date than the sixth century; and several Eastern ones, from the Liturgies of Jerusalem and Alexandria, popularly called after S. James and S. Mark, and traceable, in their "main order and substance," to the second century[b]; from

[b] Cf. Palmer, Orig. Lit. i. 43, 105; Neale, Introd. to Hist. of Eastern Ch., i. 317. It is well known that S. James' Liturgy is the parent of S. Basil's, and so of S. Chrysostom's, and of a great number of Syrian forms. The Armenian form is akin to S. Chrysostom's. Egypt has the Greek Liturgy of S. Mark, parallel to the Coptic Cyrilline, and to the Ethiopic; and two inferior Coptic forms, called after S. Basil and S. Gregory. A third great type of Liturgy is the Ephesine, or Gallican, or S. John's; various forms of which are seen in the Gothic, Francic, and Gallican Missals edited by Thomasius, the Gallican Sacramentary edited by Mabillon, and the Mozarabic ("Arabic by adoption,") or ancient Spanish; this last being much older than the Moorish invasion of A.D. 711. (See the article on this Liturgy in Chr. Remem b., Oct. 1853.) The fourth type, which is the Roman, is called after S. Peter; although there is some reason for thinking that it was originally African, and superseded a Greek Liturgy at Rome in the third century. Mr. Neale would add a fifth type—the Persian Liturgy of SS. Adæus and Maris. It may well be supposed that these archetypal Liturgies were "the legitimate development" of the "unwritten tradition" of "the Apostles whose names they bear," respecting the mode of celebration: although they have been *written* at a post-apostolic period, and have been frequently modernized and enlarged, yet the germ of each is primæval. "The words, probably, in the most important parts, the general tenor in all portions, descending unchanged from the

some other Liturgies historically connected with these, especially the great Liturgy of S. Chrysostom, the ordinary Rite of the Greek Church; and from the Daily Office and other Services of that Church.

The sources of the compilation are mainly these:—Muratori's *Liturgia Romana Vetus;* Menard's *Liber Sacramentorum D. Gregorii;* Pamelius' *Liturgicon Latinum;* Thomasius' *Codices Sacramentorum;* Mabillon *De Liturgiâ Gallicanâ;* Mr. G. H. Forbes's Gallican Liturgies; Martene *De Antiquis Ecclesiæ Ritibus;* the Mozarabic Missal and Breviary; the Ambrosian Missal; the Sarum Missal and Breviary; Maskell's *Monumenta Ritualia;* Goar's *Euchologion;* Renaudot's *Liturgiarum Orientalium Collectio;* the *Missa Armenorum;* and Neale's editions of Ancient Eastern Liturgies.

In regard to the translation, as little freedom as possible has been taken in the way of development or paraphrase. The often-recurring word *mereamur* has not been rendered "may deserve" or "may merit," because those verbs would convey a false notion of the original[e], making it express

Apostolic authors." Neale, i. 319. "The Christian Liturgies," says an eminent living historian, "*the further we inquire, seem to remount higher in primitive antiquity.*" Merivale, Hist. Rom. vi. 276.

[e] In other words, it seems to me vain to attempt to use the word

the doctrine of "condignity;" but by such words as "may obtain," or "may be enabled to have;" not by any means with a wish to ignore the fact, that it also sometimes implies the being "fitted" to obtain, and sometimes being "rewarded" with. This latter idea, when clearly distinguished from that of *proper* merit, we find in God's language both to Abraham and to the Apostles, and express in prayer during the week preceding Advent.

One section of the volume is devoted to Prayers for the exclusive use of the Clergy, with the Latin originals in most cases prefixed. But it is hoped that other passages will also prove helpful to pastors who, in the Visitation of the Sick, desire to follow the counsel of the late Professor Blunt in his admirable Lectures, and "treasure up any prayers they may meet with, such as *ancient Litur-*

merit, with regard to Christian good works, in a sound sense: it has become the property of the extreme Roman school. Bishop Forbes, of Edinburgh, in the seventeenth century, was for retaining it; but he rejected the notion of an intrinsic condignity, in works *done by grace*, with respect to the gift of salvation, as a "hateful" error, implying that Christian holiness is what, at the best, it is not. See the fifth book of his *Considerationes*. And on the frequency with which, in old Church Latin, the word *mereri* is used for "to obtain," see Maitland's Dark Ages, p. 387, and Trench on Sacred Latin Poetry, p. 132, who says, "The implied merit, which of course originally belonged to the word, has fallen quite out of sight" in these cases. One instance is the Collect for Purity, where the sense must be, "purify our thoughts, that we may be enabled (*mereamur*) to love Thee." In several cases, of course, *mereri* is used strictly for "deserving."

gies and Sacramentaries,—a most pregnant mine,—or the devotions of worthies of the Church, may supply, which they may deem fitted for the sick chamber [d]."

Some of the Collects or other prayers here presented may also be found available for the purposes of Family Prayer.

In the present Edition some inaccuracies have been corrected, and a considerable number of new prayers inserted, especially from the Leonine Sacramentary, and from the glowing and pathetic supplications of the ancient Spanish Church. In the arrangement of the prayers, also, some changes have been made with a view to greater facility in the use of the book. The "Prayers on the Incarnation," as they were called in the first Edition, are now distributed according to the seasons of Advent, Christmas, Epiphany, Lent, Passion-tide, Easter, Ascension, Whitsuntide; and the "Prayers for particular Graces" are assigned to the Trinity season, in conformity to the general character of the Church Collects for that period. But as

[d] On the Duties of the Parish Priest, p. 238. I am thankful to refer to so high an authority as the Rev. W. E. Heygate, who speaks of the first edition of this book as "a most useful companion in the Visitation of the Sick, containing a number of Collects, deep, full of ardent devotion, and very simple." (The Good Shepherd, 1860, p. 228.)

prayers of the latter class can never be inappropriate, so those of the former may, for the most part, be useful in carrying out, through the whole Christian year, the principle which would "teach and train men," as an accomplished writer on Liturgical subjects has expressed it[e], "to base their prayer and to build up their life upon the Articles of the Creed." Most precious is that principle amid the darkening shadows of the great controversy between Faith and Unbelief — amid the deepening intensity of that heart-searching process which presents to each one of us the Person of Jesus Christ, our Master and only Saviour, very God and very Man, and propounds the question, "Will ye also go away?" If we would give the Apostle's answer, we must remember that our religion is one and indivisible; that to separate the morals from the mysteries, the practical element, as it is called, from the element of supernatural fact and of pure doctrine, is simply to destroy the whole fabric[f]. The former, in truth, depends upon the latter; in the Creed of eighteen centuries

[e] The Rev. Philip Freeman, in the Christian Remembrancer for Jan. 1853.

[f] See Mansel's Bampton Lectures, 4th ed., pp. 162—166; Trench's Huls. Lect., 3rd ed., p. 171; Hannah's Discourses on the Fall, p. 244; Benson on Redemption, p. viii.

"lies, we believe, the very pith and marrow of the Gospel[g]." And if this be so, then surely the prayers of Christian people will be more accordant with the mind of Christ, and more instinct with a sense of the gloriousness of Christianity, in proportion as they dwell explicitly on "the great Mystery of Godliness[h]," and appeal to the manifold graces laid up for us in the Mediatorial work of the God-Man.

It is in His hand, Whose are all the good words of His ancient servants, to cause them, however poorly rendered, to "bring forth more fruit in their age," and minister to the increase of a living faith in His Incarnation among those for whom He died,—for whom He lives.

[g] "Danger, a Bond of Union;" a Visitation Sermon by the Rev. Prebendary Smith, Vicar of Crediton, (Rivingtons, 1861,) p. 18.

[h] Could words more clearly express the connection of Doctrine and Piety? See also 1 Tim. i. 5, 19, iii. 9, iv. 6; 2 Tim. i. 13; and consider the whole structure of the Epistle to the Ephesians.

University College, Oxford,
Whitsuntide, 1861.

CONTENTS.

INTRODUCTORY PRAYERS.

O GOD the Father of our Lord God and Saviour Jesus Christ, Lord, Whose Name is great, Whose nature is blissful, Whose goodness is inexhaustible, Thou God and Master of all things, Who art blessed for ever; Who sittest on the Cherubim, and art glorified by the Seraphim; before Whom stand thousands of thousands and ten thousand times ten thousand, the hosts of holy Angels and Archangels; sanctify, O Lord, our souls and bodies and spirits, and touch our apprehensions and search out our consciences, and cast out of us every evil thought, every base desire, all envy, and pride, and hypocrisy, all falsehood, all deceit, all worldly anxiety, all covetousness, vainglory, and sloth, all malice, all wrath, all anger, all remembrance of injuries, all blasphemy, and every motion of the flesh and spirit that is contrary to Thy holy will. And grant us, O Lord, the Lover of men, with freedom, without condemnation, with a pure heart and a contrite soul, without confusion of face and with sanctified lips, boldly to call upon Thee, our holy God and Father Who art in heaven[a].

[a] From a Prayer in the Liturgy of S. James.

LORD our God, great, eternal, wonderful in glory, Who keepest covenant and promises for those that love Thee with their whole heart; Who art the Life of all, the Help of those that flee unto Thee, the Hope of those who cry unto Thee; cleanse us from our sins, secret and open, and from every thought displeasing to Thy goodness,—cleanse our bodies and souls, our hearts and consciences, that with a pure heart and a clear soul, with perfect love and calm hope, we may venture confidently and fearlessly to pray unto Thee[b].

LORD, we beseech Thee, let Thy favour be present to Thy people who supplicate Thee; that what by Thy inspiration they faithfully ask, by Thy speedy bounty they may obtain; through Jesus Christ our Lord[c].

WE beseech Thee, O Lord, to look upon Thy servants, whom Thou hast enabled to put their trust in Thee; and grant them both to ask such things as shall please Thee, and also to obtain what they ask; through Jesus Christ our Lord[d].

O LORD our God, Who alone foreseest and bestowest things needful for our salvation; do Thou both bestow, we pray Thee, on our souls the

[b] From a Prayer in the Coptic Liturgy of S. Basil.
[c] Leonine Sacramentary. [d] Ibid.

hearty desire of imploring Thy mercy, and graciously vouchsafe us what will be for our good; through Jesus Christ our Lord[e].

WE beseech Thee, O Lord, vouchsafe us an unceasing perseverance in praying unto Thee; that as Thou dost not forsake us when we are bowed down in tribulation, so Thou mayest cherish us with more abundant grace when we continually beseech Thy Majesty; through Jesus Christ our Lord[f].

LET the prayers of Thy suppliants, O Lord, come up to the ears of Thy mercy; and that we may obtain what we ask, make us ever to ask what pleases Thee; through Jesus Christ our Lord[g].

WE beseech Thee, O Lord, to govern the hearts of Thy faithful servants; and that they may by Thy bounty obtain Thy good things, grant first of all that their own wills may be good; through Jesus Christ our Lord[h].

WE beseech Thee, O Lord, make us subject unto Thee with a ready will, and evermore stir up our wills to make supplication unto Thee; through Jesus Christ our Lord[i].

[e] Leonine. [f] Ibid.

[g] Ibid. This is the original form of our Collect for the tenth Sunday after Trinity. In the Gelasian Sacramentary it assumed its present form. See Muratori, Lit. Rom. i. 381, 689.

[h] Leonine. [i] Gelasian Sacramentary.

GRANT, O Lord, we beseech Thee, such a heart unto Thy people, that as they are brought together by their necessities to seek Thy favour, they may by their free will also become devoted to Thy Majesty; through Jesus Christ our Lord[k].

O GOD of hope, the true Light of faithful souls, and perfect Brightness of the blessed, Who art verily the Light of Thy Church, grant that our hearts may both render Thee a worthy prayer, and alway glorify Thee with the offering of praises; through Jesus Christ our Lord[l].

BE present, O Lord, to Thy faithful people; and as Thou dost in Thy compassion vouchsafe them a hearty desire to pray, grant them, O Most Loving, the aid of Thy comfort; through Jesus Christ our Lord[m].

O GOD, the Life of the faithful, the Bliss of the righteous, mercifully receive the prayers of Thy suppliants, that the souls which thirst for Thy promises may evermore be filled from Thine abundance; through Jesus Christ our Lord[n].

[k] Gelasian. [l] Ibid. [m] Ibid. [n] Ibid.

DAILY MORNING PRAYERS.

FROM the night our spirit awaketh unto Thee, O God, for Thy precepts are a light unto us. Teach us, O God, Thy righteousness, Thy commandments, and Thy judgments. Enlighten the eyes of our mind, that we sleep not in sins unto death. Drive away all darkness from our hearts. Vouchsafe us the Sun of Righteousness. Guard our life from all reproach by the seal of Thy Holy Spirit. Guide our steps into the way of peace. Grant us to behold the dawn and the day with joyfulness, that we may send up to Thee our prayers at eventide[a].

WE give Thee thanks, Lord God of our salvation, because Thou doest all things for the good of our life, that we may alway look steadfastly unto Thee, the Saviour and Benefactor of our souls; for Thou hast refreshed us in the night

[a] Day-break Office of Eastern Church.

past, and raised us up from our beds, and brought us to worship Thy glorious Name. Wherefore we beseech Thee, O Lord, give us grace and power that we may be accounted worthy to sing praise to Thee with understanding, and to pray to Thee without ceasing, in fear and trembling working out our salvation, through the aid of Thy Christ[p].

SHINE into our hearts, O loving Master, by the pure light of the knowledge of Thyself; and open the eyes of our mind to the contemplation of Thine Evangelic teaching, and put into us the fear of Thy blessed commandments; that trampling down all carnal appetites, we may follow a spiritual life, thinking and doing all things according to Thy good pleasure. For Thou art our sanctification and our illumination, and to Thee we render glory, Father, Son, and Holy Spirit, now and ever, and unto ages of ages[q].

O GOD, Who dividest the day from the night, separate our deeds from the gloom of darkness, that ever meditating on things holy, we may continually live in Thy light; through Jesus Christ our Lord[r].

WE give Thee thanks, Holy Lord, Father Almighty, everlasting God, Who hast been pleased to bring us through the night to the hours

[p] Day-break Office of Eastern Church. [q] Ibid. [r] Leonine.

of morning; we pray Thee to grant us to pass this day without sin, so that at eventide we may again give thanks to Thee; through Jesus Christ our Lord[s].

LOOK mercifully, O Lord, on the morning prayers of Thy suppliants, and enlighten with Thy healing goodness the secrets of our heart; that no dark desires may have possession of those whom the light of heavenly grace has renewed; through Jesus Christ our Lord[t].

SEND forth, O Lord, we pray Thee, Thy light into our hearts; that we may perceive the light of Thy commandments, and, walking in Thy way, may fall into no error; through Jesus Christ our Lord[u].

O GOD, Who by the light of Thy Word scatterest away the darkness of ignorance, increase in our hearts the power of faith which Thou hast given; that no temptations may avail to quench the fire which Thy grace hath caused to be enkindled; through Jesus Christ our Lord[x].

WE beseech Thee, O Lord, in Thy loving kindness, to pour Thy holy light into our souls;

[s] Gelasian. Probably the form from which our third Collect was derived, *through* another Collect in the Gregorian Sacramentary, as edited by Menard. But this latter Collect is omitted by Muratori.

[t] Gelasian.

[u] Ibid. In the Gregorian book, this Collect has the following introduction: "Almighty and everlasting God, with Whom nothing is obscure, nothing dark;" and the reading is not '*luce*,' but '*lege* mandatorum.' Murat. ii. 234.

[x] Gelasian.

that we may ever be devoted to Thee, by Whose wisdom we were created, and by Whose providence we are governed; through Jesus Christ our Lord[y].

LET our prayer, O Lord, come before Thee in the morning. Thou didst take upon Thee our feeble and suffering nature; grant us to pass this day in gladness and peace, without stumbling and without stain; that reaching the eventide without any temptation, we may praise Thee the eternal King: through Thy mercy, O our God, Who art blessed, and dost live, and govern all things, world without end[z].

[y] Gelasian.
[z] Mozarabic. A common ending of Mozarabic Collects: compare the ending of the prayer, "O merciful God," in our Office of Public Baptism.

DAILY

EVENING PRAYERS.

IN the evening, and morning, and noonday, we praise Thee, we bless Thee, we thank Thee, and pray Thee, Master of all, to direct our prayer as incense before Thee; and let not our hearts turn away to words or thoughts of wickedness, but rescue us from all things that hurt our souls. For to Thee, Lord, Lord, our eyes look up, and our hope is in Thee. Confound us not, O our God[a].

O LORD our God, Who didst bow the heavens, and come down for the salvation of mankind, look upon Thy servants and Thine inheritance. For to Thee, the awful and benignant Judge, Thy servants have bowed the head and stooped the neck, looking for no help of man, but waiting for Thy pardon and salvation. Guard them at all times, and this evening, and in the ensuing night, from every foe, from every adverse working of the devil, from idle thoughts and wicked imaginations[b].

[a] Vespers of Eastern Church. The "Prayer of entrance," just before the hymn, "O cheerful light." Euchol., p. 38.

[b] Vespers of Eastern Church. Towards the end of the service occurs this prayer, which is called that of "Bending the head."

O LORD our God, refresh us with quiet sleep, when we are wearied with the day's labour; that being assisted with the help which our weakness needs, we may be devoted to Thee both in body and mind; through Jesus Christ our Lord[c].

BE present, O Lord, to our prayers, and protect us by day and night; that in all successive changes of times we may ever be strengthened by Thine unchangeableness; through Jesus Christ our Lord[d].

ALMIGHTY and everlasting God, at evening, and morning, and noonday, we humbly beseech Thy Majesty, that Thou wouldst drive from our hearts the darkness of sins, and make us to come to the true Light, which is Christ; through Jesus Christ our Lord[e].

THINE is the day, O Lord, and Thine is the night: grant that the Sun of righteousness may abide in our hearts, to drive away the darkness of wicked thoughts; through Jesus Christ our Lord[f].

WE give Thee thanks, O Lord, Who hast preserved us through the day. We give Thee thanks, Who wilt preserve us through the night. Bring us, we beseech Thee, O Lord, in safety to

[c] Leonine. [d] Ibid. [e] Gelasian.
[f] Ibid. This Collect comes next after our third evening Collect in the Gelasian book. Murat. i. 745.

the morning hours; that Thou mayest receive our praise at all times; through Jesus Christ our Lord[g].

O GOD, Who by making the evening to succeed the day, hast bestowed the gift of repose on human weakness; grant, we beseech Thee, that while we enjoy these timely blessings, we may acknowledge Him from Whom they come[h].

O LORD God, the Life of mortals, the Light of the faithful, the Strength of those who labour, and the Repose of the dead; grant us a tranquil night free from all disturbance; that after an interval of quiet sleep, we may, by Thy bounty, at the return of light, be endued with activity from the Holy Spirit, and enabled in security to render thanks to Thee[i].

[g] Gelasian. [h] Mozarabic. [i] Ibid.

FOR A

SUNDAY OR HOLY-DAY MORNING.

WE render Thee thanksgiving upon thanksgiving[k], Lord our God, Father of our Lord God and Saviour Jesus Christ, by all means, at all times, in all places. For Thou hast sheltered, assisted, supported, and led us on through the time past of our life, and brought us to this hour. And we pray and beseech Thee, O Good and Loving, grant us to pass this holy day, and all the time of our life, without sin; with all joy, health, salvation, sanctification, and fear of Thee. But all envy, all fear, all temptation, all the working of Satan, all conspiracy of wicked men, do Thou drive away, O God, from us, and from Thy holy Catholic and Apostolic Church. Supply us with things good and profitable. Whereinsoever we have sinned against Thee, in word, or deed, or thought, be Thou pleased in Thy love and goodness to pass it over; and forsake us not, O God, who hope in Thee, neither lead us into temptation, but deliver us from the evil one, and from his works, by the

[k] εὐχαριστοῦμεν Σοι καὶ ὑπερευχαριστοῦμεν.

grace, and compassion, and benignity of Thine Only-begotten Son[l].

THE day of Resurrection has dawned upon us, the day of true light and life, wherein Christ, the Life of believers, arose from the dead. Let us give abundant thanks and praise to God, that while we solemnly celebrate the day of our Lord's Resurrection, He may be pleased to bestow on us quiet peace and special gladness; so that being protected from morning to night by His favouring mercy, we may rejoice in the gift of our Redeemer[m].

IN this hour of this day fill us, O Lord, with Thy mercy, that rejoicing throughout the whole day we may take delight in Thy praise; through Jesus Christ our Lord[n].

[l] From a Prayer in the Liturgy of S. Mark.
[m] Mozarabic. [n] Sarum.

FOR A

SUNDAY OR HOLY-DAY EVENING.

BLESSED art Thou, Almighty Master, Who hast granted us to pass through this day, and to reach the beginning of the night. Hear our prayers, and those of all Thy people; and forgive us our sins voluntary and involuntary, and accept our evening supplications, and send down on Thine inheritance the fulness of Thy mercy and Thy compassion. Compass us about with Thy holy Angels, arm us with the armour of Thy righteousness, fence us round with Thy truth, guard us with Thy power. Deliver us from every assault and every device of the adversary; and grant us to pass this evening and the ensuing night, and all the days of our life, in fulness of peace and holiness, without sin and stumbling. For it is Thine to pity and to save, O Christ our God [a].

GRANT us, O Lord, to rejoice in beholding the bliss of Thy Jerusalem, and to be carried in her bosom with perpetual gladness; that as she is the home of the multitude of the Saints, we also may

[a] From a Prayer in the Pentecost Vespers of the Eastern Church.

be counted worthy to have our portion within her; and that Thine Only-begotten Son, the Prince and Saviour of all, may in this world graciously relieve His afflicted, and hereafter in His kingdom be the everlasting Comfort of His redeemed [p].

[p] Mozarabic.

PRAYERS FOR SACRED SEASONS.

Advent.

STIR up, O Lord, Thy power, and come; and mercifully fulfil that which Thou hast promised to Thy Church unto the end of the world [q].

STIR up, we beseech Thee, O Lord, our hearts to prepare the ways of Thine Only-begotten Son; that by His Advent we may be enabled to serve Thee with purified minds; through the same Jesus Christ our Lord [r].

WE beseech Thee, O Lord, to purify our consciences by Thy daily visitation; that when Thy Son our Lord cometh, He may find in us a mansion prepared for Himself; through the same Jesus Christ our Lord [s].

MAKE us, we beseech Thee, O Lord our God, watchful and heedful in awaiting the Coming of Thy Son Christ our Lord; that when He shall come and knock, He may find us not sleeping in sins, but awake, and rejoicing in His praises; through the same Jesus Christ our Lord [t].

[q] Gelasian. [r] Ibid. [s] Ibid. [t] Ibid.

WE beseech Thee, Almighty God, let our souls enjoy this their desire, to be enkindled by Thy Spirit; that being filled, as lamps, by the Divine gift, we may shine like blazing lights before the presence of Thy Son Christ at His Coming; through the same Jesus Christ our Lord[u].

WE beseech Thee, O Lord our God, let us all rejoice with upright hearts, being gathered together in the unity of faith; that at the Coming of Thy Son our Saviour, we may go forth undefiled to meet Him, in the company of His Saints; through the same Jesus Christ our Lord[x].

WE beseech Thee, Almighty God, to behold our prayers, and to pour out upon us Thy loving tenderness; that we who are afflicted by reason of our sins may be refreshed by the Advent of our Saviour; through the same Jesus Christ our Lord[y].

WE beseech Thee, O Lord our God, to gird up the loins of our mind by Thy Divine power; that at the Coming of our Lord Jesus Christ Thy Son, we may be found worthy of the banquet of eternal life; through the same Jesus Christ our Lord[z].

[u] Gelasian. [x] Ibid. [y] Ibid. [z] Ibid.

GRANT, we beseech Thee, Almighty God, this grace unto Thy people, to wait with all vigilance for the Coming of Thine Only-begotten Son; that as He, the Author of our salvation, taught us, we may prepare our souls like blazing lamps to meet Him, through the same Jesus Christ our Lord[a].

INCLINE, O Lord, Thy merciful ears to our voice, and illuminate the darkness of our hearts by the light of Thy visitation; Who livest and reignest with the Father and the Holy Ghost, one God, world without end[b].

MAKE us, O Lord, to abhor our own evils with our whole heart; that at the Coming of Thy Son our Lord, we may be enabled to receive His good things, through the same Jesus Christ our Lord[c].

MERCIFULLY hear, O Lord, the prayers of Thy people; that as they rejoice in the Advent of Thine only-begotten Son according to the flesh, so when He cometh a second time in His Majesty, they may receive the reward of eternal life; through the same Jesus Christ our Lord[d].

[a] Gelasian.
[b] Ibid. This was substantially our Collect for the Third Sunday in Advent, until 1661. [c] Gelasian. [d] Ibid.

GRANT, we beseech Thee, Almighty God, that the coming solemnity of our redemption may both bestow upon us assistance for this present life, and also enrich us with the bliss of life eternal; through Jesus Christ our Lord[e].

BE Thou to us, O Lord, a crown of glory in the day when Thou shalt come to judge the world by fire; that Thou mayest graciously clothe us here with the robe of righteousness, and hereafter with the perfection of a glorious liberty; through Thy mercy, &c.[f]

COME to deliver us, O Lord God of hosts; turn us again, and shew Thy face, and we shall be saved; so that being cleansed by Thy mercy with the gift of worthy repentance, we may be enabled to stand before Thee in the judgment; through Thy mercy, &c.[g]

O CHRIST our God, Who wilt come to judge the world in the Manhood which Thou hast assumed, we pray Thee to sanctify us wholly, that in the day of Thy Coming our whole spirit, soul, and body may so revive to a fresh life in Thee, that we may live and reign with Thee for ever[h].

O LORD God, Father Almighty, purify the secrets of our hearts, and mercifully wash out

[e] Gelasian. [f] Mozarabic. [g] Ibid. [h] Ibid.

all the stains of sin; and grant, O Lord, that being cleansed from our crimes by the benediction of Thy tenderness, we may without any terror await the fearful and terrible Coming of Jesus Christ our Lord[i].

O GOD, Who didst look on man when he had fallen down into death, and resolve to redeem him by the Advent of Thine Only-begotten Son; grant, we beseech Thee, that they who confess His glorious Incarnation may also be admitted to the fellowship of Him, their Redeemer; through the same Jesus Christ our Lord[k].

O WISDOM, that camest out of the mouth of the Most High, reaching from one end to another, mightily and sweetly ordering all things; Come to teach us the way of understanding.

O Adonai, and Leader of the house of Israel, Who didst appear to Moses in the flame of the burning bush, and gavest the Law on Sinai; Come to deliver us with an outstretched arm.

O Root of Jesse, Who standest for an ensign to the people; before Whom kings shall shut their mouths, Whom nations shall entreat; Come to deliver us now, tarry not.

O Key of David, and Sceptre of the house of Israel, Who openest and no man shutteth, and shut-

[i] Gallican Sacramentary. [k] Ambrosian.

test and no man openeth, Come and bring forth the prisoner out of the prison-house, where he sitteth in darkness and the shadow of death.

O Day-spring, Splendour of the eternal Light, and Sun of Righteousness; Come and enlighten those who sit in darkness and the shadow of death.

O King of Gentiles, Thou Whom they long for, and Corner-stone that makest both one; Come and save man, Whom Thou formedst out of the clay.

O Emmanuel, our King and Law-giver, the Expected One of the Gentiles, and their Saviour; Come to save us, O Lord our God[l].

Christmas.

O GOD, Who makest us glad with the yearly expectation of our redemption, grant that as we joyfully receive Thine Only-begotten Son as our Redeemer, we may also see Him without fear when He cometh as our Judge; even our Lord, who with Thee, &c.[m]

GRANT, O merciful God, that for the reception of the transcendent mystery of Thy Son's Nativity, the minds of believers may be prepared, and also the hearts of unbelievers subdued; through the same Jesus Christ our Lord[n].

[l] Sarum. Seven of the great antiphons sung before *Magnificat* on the last days of Advent, beginning on Dec. 16; see our Calendar.
[m] Gelasian. This was the Collect for the First Communion on Christmas Day in the Liturgy of 1549, with only a few alterations.
[n] Gelasian.

O GOD, Who hast made this most sacred night to shine with the illumination of the True Light; grant, we beseech Thee, that as we have known the mystery of that Light upon earth, we may also perfectly enjoy it in heaven; through the same Jesus Christ our Lord [o].

(The above Collects may be said on Christmas Eve.)

GRANT, O merciful God, that He Who was born this day to be the Saviour of the world, as He is the Author of our divine birth, so may be Himself the Bestower of our immortality; through the same Jesus Christ our Lord [p].

ALMIGHTY and everlasting God, Who hast willed that on the Nativity of our Lord Jesus Christ, Thy Son, should depend the beginning and the completion of all religion; grant us, we beseech Thee, to be reckoned as a portion of Him, on Whom is built the whole salvation of mankind; Who with Thee, &c. [q]

WE beseech Thee, O Lord, bestow on Thy servants the increase of faith, hope, and charity; that as they glory in the Nativity of Thy Son our Lord, they may, by Thy governance, not feel the adversities of this world; and also that what they desire to celebrate in time, they may enjoy to all eternity; through the same Jesus Christ our Lord [r].

[o] Gelasian. [p] Leonine. [q] Ibid. [r] Ibid.

O GOD, Who art pleased to save, by the Nativity of Thy Christ, the race of man, which was mortally wounded in its chief; grant, we beseech Thee, that we may not cleave to the author of our perdition, but be transferred to the fellowship of our Redeemer; Who with Thee, &c.[s]

GRANT unto us, we pray Thee, O Lord our God, that we who rejoice to keep the feast of the Nativity of Jesus Christ our Lord, may by walking worthily of Him attain to fellowship with Him, through the same Jesus Christ our Lord[t].

GRANT, O Lord, we beseech Thee, to Thy people an inviolable firmness of faith; that as they confess Thine Only-begotten Son, the everlasting partaker of Thy glory, to have been born in our very flesh, of the Virgin Mother, they may be delivered from present adversities, and admitted into joys that shall abide; through the same Jesus Christ our Lord[u].

GRANT, we beseech Thee, O Lord our God, that Thy Church may alike apprehend both parts of the one Mystery, and adore One Christ,

[s] Leonine. [t] Ibid.

[u] Ibid. This Collect and that which follows it appear to speak the very mind of S. Leo, the steadfast maintainer of both sides of the sacred truth as to our Lord's One Person and Two Natures. They exclude alike the Nestorian severance of the Son of God from the Son of Mary, and the Eutychian absorption of His Manhood in His Godhead.

very God and very Man, neither divided from our nature nor separate from Thine essence; through the same Jesus Christ our Lord [y].

GRANT, we beseech Thee, Almighty God, that the new Birth of Thine Only-begotten Son in the flesh may set free those whom the old bondage detains under the yoke of sin; through the same Jesus Christ our Lord [z].

GRANT, we beseech Thee, O our God, that Thy family, which has been saved by the Nativity of Thy Son our Lord Jesus Christ, may also quietly repose on Him as a perpetual Redeemer, Who with Thee, &c. [a]

ALMIGHTY and everlasting God, Who by Thine Only-begotten Son hast made us to be a new creation for Thyself, preserve the works of Thy mercy, and cleanse us from all our ancient stains; that by the assistance of Thy grace we may be found in His form, in Whom our substance dwells with Thee, through the same Jesus Christ our Lord [b].

BE present, O Lord, to our supplications; and let Thy people, who were framed by Thy making and restored by Thy power, be also saved

[y] Leonine. [z] Gelasian. [a] Ibid. [b] Ibid.

by Thy continual operation, through Jesus Christ our Lord [c].

GRANT, we beseech Thee, Almighty God, that as we are bathed in the new light of Thine Incarnate Word, that which shines by faith in our minds may blaze out likewise in our actions; through the same Jesus Christ our Lord [d].

GRANT to us, Almighty God, that as Thy Salvation, wondrous with a new and heavenly light, went forth on this day's festival to redeem the world, so it may ever beam forth in the renewal of our hearts; through the same Jesus Christ our Lord [e].

MERCIFUL and most loving God, by Whose will and bounty Jesus Christ our Lord humbled Himself for this—that He might exalt the whole race of man; and descended to the depths for the purpose of lifting up the lowly; and was born, God-Man, by the Virgin, for this cause—that He might restore in man the lost celestial image; grant that Thy people may cleave unto Thee, that as Thou hast redeemed them by Thy bounty, they may ever please Thee by devoted service [f].

[c] Gelasian. [d] Gregorian. [e] Ibid. [f] Gallican Sacramentary.

BLESSED be the Lord God, Who cometh in the Name of the Lord, and hath dawned upon us; Whose Coming hath redeemed us, Whose Nativity hath enlightened us; Who by His Coming hath sought out the lost, and illuminated those who sat in darkness. Grant, therefore, O Father Almighty, that we celebrating with pious devotion the day of His Nativity, may find the day of judgment a day of mercy; that as we have known His benignity as our Redeemer, we may feel His gentle tenderness as our Judge[g].

WE give Thee thanks, O Lord our God, and bless Thee from day to day, Who hast been pleased to bring us to this Thy holy solemnity. Vouchsafe us, with Thy faithful people, in peace and quietness through many succeeding years to welcome this Thy Birth-day, through Thy mercy, &c.[h]

ALMIGHTY and everlasting God, Who hast hallowed this day by the Incarnation of Thy Word, and the Child-bearing of the Blessed Virgin Mary; grant Thy people to share in this celebration, that they who have been redeemed by Thy grace may be happy as Thine adopted children; through the same Jesus Christ our Lord[i].

[g] Mozarabic. [h] Ibid. [i] Gelasian as altered in Gregorian.

ALMIGHTY and everlasting God, the Light of the faithful and the Ruler of souls, Who hast hallowed us by the Incarnation of Thy Word, and the Child-bearing of the Blessed Virgin Mary; we beseech Thee, let the power of Thy Holy Spirit come also upon us, and the mercy of the Highest overshadow us[k].

O CHRIST, Almighty Son of God, come graciously on the day of Thy Nativity to be the Saviour of Thy people; that with Thy wonted goodness Thou mayest deliver us from all anxiety and all temporal fear, Who livest and reignest, &c.[l]

WE beseech Thee, O Lord, let our hearts be graciously enlightened by the holy radiance of Thy Son's Incarnation; that so we may escape the darkness of this world, and by His guidance attain to the country of eternal brightness; through the same Jesus Christ our Lord[m].

O GOD, Who hast made the most glorious Name of our Lord Jesus Christ, Thine Only-begotten Son, to be exceeding sweet and supremely lovable to Thy faithful servants, and tremendous and terrible to malignant spirits; mercifully grant that all who devoutly venerate this Name of Jesus on earth, may in this life receive the sweetness of holy

[k] Mozarabic. According to Lesley's emendation, which would make the first sentence rather like the preceding Collect. Miss. Moz., 19.
[l] Ambrosian. [m] Sarum, based on Gelasian.

comfort, and in the life to come attain the joy of exulting gladness and never-ending jubilation; through the same Jesus Christ our Lord [n].

Epiphany.

O GOD, Whose Only-begotten Son hath appeared in substance of our flesh; grant, we beseech Thee, that through Him Whom we have acknowledged as outwardly like unto us, we may attain an inward renewal; through the same Jesus Christ our Lord [o].

ALMIGHTY and everlasting God, Who hast made known the Incarnation of Thy Word by the testimony of a glorious star, which when the wise men beheld, they adored Thy Majesty with gifts; grant that the star of Thy righteousness may alway appear in our hearts, and our treasure consist in giving thanks to Thee; through Jesus Christ our Lord [p].

O GOD, the Enlightener of all nations, grant Thy people to enjoy perpetual peace; and pour into our hearts that radiant light which Thou didst shed into the minds of the wise men [q]; through Jesus Christ our Lord [r].

WE beseech Thee, O Lord, to enlighten Thy people, and alway set their hearts on fire with the brightness of Thy glory; that they may

[n] Sarum Missal. [o] Gelasian. [p] Ibid.
[q] Orig., "*Trium* Magorum." Mur. i. 502. [r] Gelasian.

both unceasingly acknowledge their Saviour, and truly apprehend their Lord, Who with Thee, &c. [s]

ALMIGHTY and everlasting God, the Brightness of faithful souls, Who hast consecrated this solemnity by the first-fruits of the chosen Gentiles; fill the world with Thy glory, and shew Thyself by the radiance of Thy light to the nations that are subject unto Thee; through Jesus Christ our Lord [t].

WE beseech Thee, O Lord, mercifully to correct our wanderings, and by the guiding radiance of Thy compassion to bring us to the salutary vision of Thy truth, through Jesus Christ our Lord [u].

O GOD, Who through Thine Only-begotten Son Jesus Christ our Lord hast endowed the regenerating waters with the grace which halloweth unto eternal salvation; and didst Thyself come upon Him by Thy Spirit, in the descent of the mysterious Dove on His head; grant, we beseech Thee, that there may come upon Thy whole Church a blessing which may keep us all continually safe, may unceasingly bless all classes of Thy servants, may direct the course of those who follow Thee, and

[s] Gregorian. [t] Ibid.
[u] Gothic Missal. Used in Southern Gaul; the "Gallican" being the use of Central and the "Francic" of Northern.

open the door of the heavenly kingdom to all who are waiting to enter; through Jesus Christ our Lord[v].

O GLORIOUS, holy, Almighty God, Who being ever pitiful to the manifold wanderings of mankind, didst doubtless for this end guide the Magi, who dwelt in dark superstition, by the light of a star to Thy sacred cradle, that Thou mightest kindle all men who were walking in their own errors with the desire of knowing Thee; kindle us also, we pray Thee, with the saving ardour of love for Thee, that we who have already known Thee by Thy gracious illumination, may be enabled to cleave to Thee for ever[w].

GRANT, O Almighty God, that we may be able continually to shake off the yoke of Egyptian servitude and sin, and to appear before Thy Majesty in our heavenly country; through Jesus Christ our Lord[x].

Lent, or other Fast-days.

GRANT, O Lord, to Thy faithful people that they may enter on the venerable solemnity of this fast with fitting piety, and go through it with undisturbed devotion; through Jesus Christ our Lord[y].

[v] Gothic. [w] Mozarabic. [x] Ambrosian. [y] Gregorian.

GRANT us, O Lord, to enter on the service of our Christian warfare with holy fasting; that as we are to fight against spiritual powers of wickedness, we may be fortified by the aid of self-denial; through Jesus Christ our Lord [z].

O GOD, Who by Thy Word dost marvellously work out the reconciliation of mankind; grant, we beseech Thee, that by the holy fast we may both be subjected to Thee with all our hearts, and be united to each other in prayer to Thee; through Jesus Christ our Lord [a].

O GOD, Who in Thy deep counsel and foresight for mankind, hast appointed holy fasts, whereby the hearts of the weak might receive salutary healing; do Thou purify our souls and bodies, O Saviour of body and soul, O loving Bestower of eternal happiness! through Jesus Christ our Lord [b].

WE beseech Thee, O Lord, let Thy gracious favour carry us through the fast which we have begun; that as we observe it by bodily discipline, so we may be able to fulfil it with sincerity of mind; through Jesus Christ our Lord [c].

GRANT to us, O Almighty God, that by the annual exercise of Lenten observances we may

[z] Leonine. [a] Gelasian. [b] Ibid. [c] Ibid.

advance in knowledge of the mystery of Christ, and follow His mind by conduct worthy of our calling, through the same Jesus Christ our Lord[d].

WE beseech Thee, O Lord, to sanctify our fasts, and mercifully to grant us forgiveness of all our sins, through Jesus Christ our Lord[e].

VOUCHSAFE us, O Lord, we beseech Thee, the aid of Thy grace; that being intent, as becomes us, on fasting and prayer, we may be delivered from bodily and spiritual enemies; through Jesus Christ our Lord[f].

GRANT, we beseech Thee, O Lord, Eternal King of all, that being purified by the sacred fast, we may come with sincere minds to partake of Thy holy things; through Jesus Christ our Lord[g].

GRANT, we beseech Thee, O Lord, that renewing our sacred observances with annual devotion, we may please Thee both in body and soul; through Jesus Christ our Lord[h].

WE beseech Thee, O Lord, that our earnest devotion may become fruitful through Thy grace; for then shall our fast be profitable to us, if it is well-pleasing to Thy loving-kindness; through Jesus Christ our Lord[i].

[d] Gelasian. [e] Ibid. [f] Ibid. [g] Ibid. [h] Ibid. [i] Ibid.

WE beseech Thee, O Lord, give a salutary effect to our fasting, that the mortification of our flesh may prove the nourishment of our souls; through Jesus Christ our Lord[k].

O GOD, Who didst spare the Ninevites when they fasted for their sins; we humbly beseech Thee that in this our fast Thou wouldest, of Thine accustomed mercy, vouchsafe to us also Thy forgiveness; through Jesus Christ our Lord[l].

Several of the following penitential Collects may be found suitable for ordinary use.

O GOD, if Thou shouldest determine to render to us what we deserve, we must sooner perish than endure our deserved punishment; we therefore pray Thee mercifully to forgive our wanderings; and that we may be able to be converted to Thy commandments, do Thou go before us with abundant mercy; through Jesus Christ our Lord[m].

WE beseech Thee, O Lord, in Thy forgiving love, turn away what we deserve for our sins, nor let our offences prevail before Thee, but let Thy mercy alway rise up to overcome them; through Jesus Christ our Lord[n].

O GOD, Who sufferest not that offenders should perish without being enabled to be converted

[k] Gelasian. [l] Old Gallican Missal.
[m] Leonine. [n] Ibid.

and live[o], we beseech Thee to suspend the vengeance due to our sins, and mercifully grant that no dissembling on our part may increase our punishment, but rather that amendment may avail for our pardon; through Jesus Christ our Lord[p].

BE present, O Lord, to our supplications; nor let Thy merciful clemency be far away from Thy servants[q]. Heal our wounds, forgive our sins, that being severed from Thee by no iniquities, we may be able evermore to cleave to Thee our Lord[r].

THOU Who didst bring home the lost sheep to the fold on Thy shoulders, Who wast appeased by the prayers and confession of the publican, do Thou, O Lord, be favourable also to Thy servants, do Thou graciously attend to their prayers[s].

MAY Thy mercy, O Lord, we beseech Thee, be beforehand with Thy servants, and all their iniquities be blotted out by Thy speedy pardon; through Jesus Christ our Lord[t].

[o] "Qui delinquentes perire non pateris, *donec* convertantur et vivant." A remarkable use of *until*.

[p] Leonine.

[q] This collect occurs twice in the Gelasian: in one case, as a prayer over a single penitent, Murat. i. 504; in the other case it uses the first person plural, Murat. i. 708.

[r] Gelasian. [s] Ibid. [t] Ibid.

O GOD, the most gracious Maker and most merciful Restorer of mankind, Who, when man, by the envy of the Devil[w], was cast down from eternal life, didst redeem him with the Blood of Thine Only Son; give life to Thy servants, whose death Thou dost in no wise desire; and as Thou dost not leave them when they are astray, so do Thou receive them when they are brought back. Let the sorrowful sighings of Thy servants move Thy pity. Do Thou heal their wounds; do Thou extend Thy saving hand to the prostrate, lest Thy Church should be despoiled of any portion of her body; lest Thy flock should suffer loss; lest those who were born again in the salutary laver should be possessed by the second death. Spare Thou those who confess; that in this mortal life they may, by Thy help, so mourn over their sins, that in the day of the dreadful judgment they may escape the sentence of eternal damnation, and may know neither the terrors of the darkness nor the fury of the flame[x]; and that having returned from the path of error to the way of righteousness, they may be pierced with no more wounds, but may retain in fulness and perpetuity both what Thy grace hath

[w] Wisdom ii. 24.

[x] "Quod *stridet in* flammis." This expression occurs in the Commendation of a departing soul, composed by Peter Damian, and adopted by the Roman Church. See a translation of it in Williams on the Passion, p. 441.

vouchsafed, and what Thy mercy hath restored; through the same our Lord Jesus Christ[y].

O GOD, beneath Whose eyes every heart trembles, and all consciences are afraid; be merciful to the groanings of all, and heal the wounds of all; that as not one of us is free from fault, so not one may be shut out from pardon; through Jesus Christ our Lord[z].

ALMIGHTY and merciful God, Who willest not the souls of sinners to perish, but their faults; restrain the anger which we deserve, and pour out upon us the clemency which we entreat, that through Thy mercy we may pass from mourning into joy; through Jesus Christ our Lord[a].

WE beseech Thee, O Lord, in Thy clemency, to shew us Thine unspeakable mercy; that Thou mayest both set us free from our sins, and rescue us from the punishments which for our sins we deserve; through Jesus Christ our Lord[b].

O GOD, Who purifiest the hearts of those who confess their sins unto Thee, and absolvest the self-accusing conscience from all bonds of iniquity;

[y] From a Gelasian prayer as developed in the Gregorian book, and very widely used in the Western Church: see extracts from the Pontifical of Archbishop Egbert of York, (*circ.* 750,) and other Rituals, in Martene, i. 767, seqq. See too the Sarum Missal, 72, "In cœnâ Domini."

[z] Gelasian.

[a] Ibid.

[b] Ibid. Anciently used in the Sarum Litany, and in the English Litany of 1544.

give pardon to the guilty, and vouchsafe healing to the wounded, that they may receive remission of all sins, and persevere henceforward in sincere devotion, and sustain no loss of everlasting redemption; through Jesus Christ our Lord[c].

O GOD the Trinity, Whose Name is ineffable, Who purifiest the cavern of man's heart from vices, and makest it whiter than the snow; bestow on us Thy compassions; renew in our inward parts, we pray Thee, Thy Holy Spirit, by Whom we may be able to show forth Thy praise; that being strengthened by the righteous and princely Spirit, we may attain a place in the heavenly Jerusalem; through Jesus Christ our Lord[d].

BEFORE Thine eyes, O Lord, I stand guilty by the witness of my own conscience. I hardly dare to ask what I do not deserve to obtain. For Thou, Lord, knowest our doings. We blush to confess what we fear not to commit. Unto Thee, after falling into sin, I return from my wanderings; before Thee I lie sorely wounded; worthless as I am, my only relief is in Thee, O good Physician! Everywhere Thou findest us; therefore unto Thee we flee, because from Thee we cannot escape. Let Thy forgiveness comfort those whom their guilt

[c] Gelasian.
[d] Gallican. A specimen of prayers based on the *Miserere*. The Mozarabic Breviary has others, (e.g. pp. 150, 231).

terrifies. We plead guilty before Thee, O Lord; spare us, because Thou art kind. We know that unless Thou pardon, Thou mayest justly punish us. But with Thee is great mercy, and overflowing readiness to forgive. Let Thy loving-kindness, from which we hope everything, not impute to us that wherein we have offended, but look upon that which we ask[e].

O GOD, Who desirest not the death, but the repentance of sinners, reject not from Thy tender love my wretched self, a frail sinner; nor look to my sins and crimes, and my unclean and base thoughts, whereby I am wofully disunited from Thy will; but look Thou to Thine own mercy[f].

RECEIVE my confession, O my only Hope of Salvation, Jesus Christ, my Lord and God. For in . . . . I am lost, and altogether in thought, word, and deed, and in all evils, I am overwhelmed. Thou Who justifiest the ungodly and quickenest the dead, Lord my God, justify me and revive me. Save me, O Lord, King of eternal glory, Who canst save. Grant me to will and to do, and to accomplish, what is pleasing to Thee, and profitable to myself; give me aid in distress, consolation in

[e] From various "Apologiæ Sacerdotis" in Menard's Gregorian Sacramentary.

[f] From an old Missa annexed to the Gregorian book in Menard's edition.

persecution, and strength in all temptation; vouchsafe me pardon for past evils, amendment of present evils, and be pleased to send me protection against evils to come. Thine it is to give the sinner a stricken heart and a fountain of tears. It is mine, if Thou shalt vouchsafe it, to weep for my sins; it is Thine to efface them speedily, as a cloud. I beseech Thee, O Lord, to forget my sins, and to remember Thy mercies. O Christ, spare me, pity me, not according to my deserts, but according to Thy mercy. Do not despise me a sinner. Do not cast me away, but receive me according to Thy word, that I may live, and not be disappointed of my hope. Give me a fountain of tears, O Fountain of life. My hope of salvation is in no works of mine; but my soul hangs simply on the boundlessness of Thy love, and confides in the multitude of Thy mercy[g].

ALMIGHTY and everlasting God, by Whom that begins to be which was not, and that which lay hid is made visible, cleanse away the folly of our heart, and purify us from our secret vices; that we may be able to serve Thee, O Lord, with a pure mind; through Jesus Christ our Lord[h].

[g] From the Missal first published by Matthias Illyricus, 1557, and supposed by Mabillon and Martene to be a Pontifical Missa, according to the Roman rite, for a monastic church. Parts of this prayer are found in Menard's edition of the Gregorian Sacr., pp. 245, 262.

[h] Gelasian.

HEAR our prayer, O Lord, and listen to our groanings, for we acknowledge our iniquities, and lay open our sins before Thee. Against Thee, O God, have we sinned; to Thee we make our confession, and implore forgiveness. Turn Thy face again, O Lord, upon Thy servants whom Thou hast redeemed with Thine own Blood. Spare us, we pray Thee, and vouchsafe pardon to our sins, and be pleased to extend to us Thy loving-kindness and Thy mercy[i].

O GOOD Jesus, Who didst enable Lazarus at the sound of Thy voice to rise from the tomb, grant us to hear Thy voice in our souls, and to rise through grace from the depth of our own sin[k].

CLEANSE, O Lord, our consciences by the sincere confession of the Catholic Faith, and by continual contrition of heart; that we may always be heard by Thee in heaven, when we call to Thee for pardon of sins on earth[l].

MAY forgiveness, O Lord, we beseech Thee, proceed from the Most High. May it succour us in our misery; may it cleanse us from our offences; may it be granted to penitents; may it plead for mourners; may it bring back those who wander from the faith; may it raise up those who are fallen

[i] Mozarabic. [k] Ibid. [l] Ibid.

into sins; may it reconcile us to the Father; may it confirm us with the grace of Christ; may it conform us to the Holy Spirit[m].

Passion-tide[n].

IT is meet and right that we should give thanks to Thee, O Lord God, through Jesus Christ Thy Son, Who, being God Eternal, was pleased to become Man for our salvation. O the one, peerless, manifold Mystery of our Saviour! For He, being one and the same, God most high, and perfect Man, both supreme High Priest and most sacred Sacrifice, according to His Divine power created all things, according to His human condition delivered man; by virtue of His Sacrifice He atoned for the polluted, in right of His Priesthood He reconciled the alienated. O the one peerless Mystery of redemption! wherein those ancient wounds were healed by the Lord's new medicine, and the judgment passed before on the first man was rescinded by the privileges of our Saviour. The one in self-indulgence extended his hands to the tree, the other patiently fitted His to the Cross; therefore deservedly did

[m] Mozarabic. In the original this is part of a Good-Friday Litany, of which the word *Indulgentia* forms the burden. Miss. Moz. 171; Brev. 365.

[n] The character of the prayers here translated throws considerable light on the question whether ancient Christianity regarded the death of our Lord as the greatest of "moral acts," or as a true and perfect satisfaction. See also the Eucharistic Prayers.

the punishment borne by innocence become the discharge of the debtor, for with good right are debts remitted to debtors when discharged on their behalf by Him Who owed nothing[o].

ALMIGHTY and everlasting God, Who restorest us by the blessed Passion of Thy Christ, preserve in us the works of Thy mercy; that by the celebration of this Mystery our lives may be continually devout; through the same Jesus Christ our Lord[p].

WE beseech Thee, O Lord, purify Thy family, and cleanse it from all contagion of wickedness; that the vessels which have been redeemed by their Lord's Passion may never again be stained by the unclean spirit, but may be possessed by everlasting salvation; through the same Jesus Christ our Lord[q].

REMEMBER Thy compassions, O Lord, and sanctify with eternal protection Thy servants, for whom Christ Thy Son by His Blood appointed unto us the Paschal mystery; through the same Jesus Christ our Lord[r].

O GOD, Who by the Passion of Thy Christ our Lord hast dissolved that hereditary death of

[o] From an ancient Gallican Missa published by Mone. See Mone's *Messen*, and the Rev. G. Forbes's valuable edition of Gallican Liturgies. Of this series of Missæ part is Ante-Nicene, belonging to times when persecution silenced the Church's *citharæ*.

[p] Leonine. [q] Ibid. [r] Gelasian.

the ancient sin, to which the whole race of Adam's posterity had succeeded; grant that having been made conformable unto Him, as we by necessity of nature have borne the image of the earthly, so by the sanctification of grace we may bear the image of the Heavenly, even of Christ our Lord; Who with Thee, &c.[s]

GRANT, we beseech Thee, Almighty God, that we who amid so many adversities have fainted through our own infirmity, may be relieved by the intervention of the Passion of Thine only-begotten Son; through the same Jesus Christ our Lord[t].

GRANT, we beseech Thee, Almighty God, that we who are incessantly afflicted by our own transgressions, may be delivered by the Passion of Thine only-begotten Son; Who with Thee, &c.[u]

O GOD, Who for us hast willed Thy Son to endure the gibbet of the Cross, that Thou mightest drive away from us the power of the enemy; grant to us Thy servants to attain the grace of resurrection; through the same Jesus Christ our Lord[x].

O LOVING Wisdom of the living God, O living everlasting Word and everlasting Power of God the eternal Father,—for everlasting is Thy birth, Who art the everlasting Son of God the ever-

[s] Gelasian. [t] Gregorian. [u] Ibid. [x] Ibid.

lasting Father, and art God; without Whom is nothing, by Whom are all things; in Whom consisteth whatever is; Who art God above us, and Man for our sakes; for Thou hast willed for us to be what we are: grant us what Thou hast promised; give to us, although unworthy, what Thou hast offered to all alike; that is, that Thy Passion may be our deliverance, and Thy Death our life, and Thy Cross our redemption, and Thy Wound our healing; that being crucified with Thee, we may by Thy gift be lifted up on high to Thy Father, with Whom in bliss Thou livest and reignest, &c.[y]

O GOD, Who for our redemption hast received the Blood of Jesus Christ, destroy the works of the devil, and break through all the snares of sin; that those who have been created by a new birth may not be defiled by the old contagion[z].

LORD Jesus Christ, Who didst stretch out Thine hands on the Cross, and redeem us by Thy Blood, forgive me a sinner, for none of my thoughts are hid from Thee. Pardon I ask, pardon I hope for, pardon I trust to have. Thou Who art pitiful and merciful, spare and forgive me[a].

LORD Jesus Christ, Son of the living God, Who for our redemption willedst to be born and circumcised, and rejected by the Jews, betrayed with

[y] Old Gallican. [z] Gothic. [a] Ambrosian.

a kiss by Judas, seized, bound, and led in bonds to Annas, Caiaphas, Herod, and Pilate, and before them to be mocked, smitten with palm and fist, with the scourge and the reed; to have Thy face covered and defiled with spitting; to be crowned with thorns, accused by false witnesses, condemned, and as an innocent Lamb to be led to slaughter, bearing Thine own Cross; to be pierced through with nails, to have gall and vinegar given Thee to drink, on the Cross to die the most shameful of deaths, and to be wounded with a spear; do Thou by these Thy most sacred pains deliver us from all sins and penalties, and by Thy holy Cross bring us, miserable sinners, to that place whither Thou didst bring with Thyself the crucified robber on his late repentance; Who livest and reignest, &c.[b]

GRACIOUS Lord, Almighty, Jesus Christ, let Thy sufferings aid us, and defend us from all pain and grief, all peril and misery, all uncleanness of heart, all sin, all scandal and infamy, from evil diseases of soul and body, from sudden and unforeseen death, and from all persecution of our foes visible and invisible. For we know that in what day or hour we call to mind Thy Passion, we shall be safe. Therefore relying on Thine infinite tenderness, we beseech Thee, O most loving Saviour, by

[b] Sarum Missal; a Prayer of Innocent III.

Thy most benignant and sacred sufferings to protect us with gracious aid, and in continual tenderness to preserve us from all evil[c].

O GOD, the Son of God,—so loving, yet hated,—so forbearing, yet assaulted unto death,—Who didst show Thyself so gentle and merciful to Thy persecutors; grant that through the wounds of Thy Passion our sins may be expiated, and as in Thy humiliation Thou didst suffer death for us, so now, being glorified, bestow on us everlasting brightness[d].

O CHRIST, the Son of God, Whom the savage multitude persecuted with blind fury, and while they inflicted suffering on Thee as Man, discerned not in Thee the essence of Godhead; grant that we, confessing Thee, true God and Man, to be One Christ, may be removed far away from eternal punishment[e].

JESUS, our God, Who gavest Thy cheek to those who smote Thee, and wast for our sakes filled full with reproach[f]; grant to us Thy servants that, being instructed by the example of Thy Passion, we may be fitted alway to bear Thy sweet yoke, and learn of Thee Who art meek and lowly of heart[g].

[c] Sarum Missal; a prayer of Innocent III. [d] Mozarabic.
[e] Mozarabic. [f] Lam. iii. 30. [g] Mozarabic.

O CHRIST, Son of God, Whom God the Father gave up for all, when He received Thee as a true Sacrifice for us; receive the desires of Thy people; save those whom Thou hast redeemed; give life to those whom Thou hast delivered; suffer not those to go into everlasting anguish, whom Thou camest to redeem from perishing eternally; and grant that through Thee, Whom we believe to have been crucified for all, we may have remission of sins in this life, and everlasting joy in the life to come [h].

REMEMBER, O Jesus, the vinegar and gall, that bitter cup which Thou didst taste for the ungodly; and let the bitterness which was Thy portion be to us a cause of perpetual sweetness [i].

LORD Jesus Christ, Son of the living God, Who didst descend from heaven to earth, out of the bosom of the Father, and didst sustain five wounds upon the wood of the Cross, and shed Thy precious Blood for the remission of our sins; we humbly beseech Thee that at the day of judgment we may be set at Thy right hand, and be thought worthy to hear those sweetest words, "Come, ye blessed, into the kingdom of My Father:" Who with the same Father, &c. [k]

[h] Mozarabic. [i] Ibid. [k] Sarum Missal.

LORD Jesus Christ, Who for the redemption of the world didst ascend the wood of the Cross, that Thou mightest enlighten the whole world which lay in darkness; pour that light, we pray Thee, into our souls and bodies, whereby we may be enabled to attain to the light eternal: Who with the Father, &c.[l]

BY the shedding of the Blood of Christ our Lord, peace has been established in heaven and earth. O truly precious is the Covenant of peace, which was made by the offering of that holy Blood! not with gold, nor silver, nor gems, nor pearls, but with the Blood that gushed from the side of the Saviour. That Blood-shedding gladdened heaven, purified earth, and terrified hell[m].

The five prayers following are specially for Good Friday.

TO-DAY, O good Jesus, for us Thou didst not hide Thy Face from shame and spitting. To-day, Jesus our Redeemer, for us Thou wast mocked, buffeted by unbelievers, and crowned with thorns. To-day, O good Shepherd, Thou didst lay down Thy life on the Cross for the sheep, and wast crucified with robbers, and hadst Thy sacred hands nailed through. To-day Thou wast laid in the guarded sepulchre, and the Saints burst open their tombs. To-day, O good Jesus, put an end to our

[l] Sarum Missal.

[m] Gallican Sacramentary.

sins, that on the day of Thy Resurrection we may joyfully receive Thy holy Body, and be refreshed with Thy sacred Blood [n].

O CHRIST, the Only-begotten Son of the Unbegotten Father, Who for us wast this day slain, the Innocent for the ungodly; remember the price of Thy Blood, and blot out the sins of all Thy people; and as Thou wast pleased to endure for us reproaches, spitting, bonds, blows, the scourge, the cross, the nails, the bitter cup, death, the spear, and lastly burial; vouchsafe to us wretched ones for whom Thou didst suffer this, the infinite blessedness of the heavenly kingdom; that we who bow down in reverence for Thy Passion, may be raised up to things heavenly in the joys of Thy Resurrection [o].

O CHRIST, God, great Adonai, crucify us as it were with Thyself to this world, that Thy life may be in us: and put our sins upon Thyself to crucify them; and draw us also to Thyself, since for us Thou wast lifted up from the earth, to deliver us from the tyrant: for although by the flesh and by sins we are under the devil's power, yet we long to serve Thee, not him; and we desire to live under Thine authority, and beg to be governed by Thee, Who wast pleased by the death of the

[n] Mozarabic. [o] Ibid.

Cross to deliver us, mortals, and invaded by death. For which transcendent benefit we this day bring the service of our devotion; and now this day we humbly adore, implore, invoke Thee, that Thou, O God, eternal Might, wouldest hasten unto us. Thou Who by Thy power makest things future to be as things past, and also by Thy presence, things past to be as things present; grant that Thy Passion may be as saving to us as if it were present this day: Thou Who reignest for ever with the Father and the Holy Ghost, now begin to reign over us, Man, God, Christ Jesus, King for ever and ever[p].

DELIVERED from evil, and established continually in good, may we be able to cleave unto Thee, Jesus Christ our Lord and God. Break in pieces all the snares of our enemy; accept our fasting and hear our prayer, in these days and in all times. Grant us peace and quietness, piety, pure love, and grace, by the wounds of Thy Passion, O our God, Son of God, Who livest with God the Father, and reignest with the Holy Spirit, One God in Trinity, abiding throughout all ages[q].

SPEAK to our hearts, O Christ our Overseer; say to us, "Hail, be strong and of good courage." Thou who didst this of old, canst Thou not

[p] From a prayer for noonday on Good Friday, in the Old Gallican.
[q] Mozarabic.

do the same now? Thou canst, Thou canst indeed! for Thou art Almighty. Thou canst, O most Loving, Thou canst do what we cannot conceive; for nothing is impossible to Thee, Almighty God! Truly, O Saviour, for us Thy Body is red with Blood; Thou hast "washed Thy garment in wine, and Thy clothes in the blood of grapes;" for Thou art God alone, crucified for us, whom the old transgression gave over unto death; by Thy wound have been healed the countless wounds of our sins. And now, O loving and crucified Christ, redeem us with Thine own; save us, O loving Goodness, O God, Who reignest with the Father and the Holy Spirit, One God for ever, throughout all ages[r].

Easter.

HEAR us, O Lord, Father Almighty, through the New Adam; that being buried with Jesus Thy Son, and raised up again by His life, we may in this ensuing night of His holy Resurrection, by the grace that attends the great solemnity, by His gift and Thy blessing, and the counsel and mysterious working of the Holy Spirit, obtain absolution through Him, Who with Thee, &c.[s]

O CHRIST, be favourable to our desires and prayers, and make prosperous to us this coming night of holy Easter; that in it we may rise from

[r] Old Gallican Missal. [s] Ibid, Holy Saturday.

the dead, and pass over into life, with Thee, O Saviour of the world [t].

HEAR us, O never-failing Light, Lord our God, our only Light, the Fountain of light, the Light of Thine Angels, Thrones, Dominions, Principalities, Powers, and of all intelligent beings; Who hast created the light of Thy Saints. May our souls be lamps of Thine, kindled and illuminated by Thee. May they shine and burn with the truth, and never go out in darkness and ashes. May we be Thy house, shining from Thee, shining in Thee; may we shine and fail not; may we ever worship Thee; in Thee may we be kindled, and not be extinguished. Being filled with the splendour of Thy Son our Lord Jesus Christ, may we shine forth inwardly; may the gloom of sins be cleared away, and the light of perpetual faith abide within us [u].

IT is very meet and right, with all powers of heart and mind, and with the service of the lips, to praise the invisible God, the Father Almighty, and His Only-begotten Son our Lord Jesus Christ, Who paid the debt of Adam for us to the eternal Father, and effaced the bond of the ancient guilt

[t] Old Gallican.

[u] Mozarabic. This and the next following passage belong to forms for the solemn blessing of the great Paschal candle on Easter Eve, probably one of the oldest of Church ceremonies. The Gregorian form has been ascribed, perhaps unduly, to S. Augustine.

by the Blood poured forth in loving-kindness. For this is the Paschal festival in which that true Lamb is slain, and the door-posts hallowed by His Blood: in which first Thou didst bring our fathers, the children of Israēl, out of Egypt, and madest them to pass over the Red Sea dry-shod. This then is the night which cleared away the darkness of sin by a pillar of radiance. This is the night which now throughout the world restores to grace and unites to holiness believers in Christ, separated from worldly vices and from the gloom of sin. This is the night in which Christ broke the bonds of death, and ascended a Conqueror from the grave. For to be born had been no blessing to us, unless we could have been redeemed. O the wondrous condescension of Thy loving-kindness towards us! O the inestimable tenderness of Thy love! To redeem the servant, Thou gavest up the Son. This holy night, then, puts to flight offences, washes away sins, and restores innocence to the fallen, and joyousness to the sad. O truly blessed night, which spoiled the Egyptians and enriched the Hebrews—the night in which heaven and earth are reconciled! We pray Thee therefore, O Lord, that Thou wouldest preserve Thy servants in the peaceful enjoyment of this Easter happiness, through Jesus Christ our Lord[1].

[1] Gregorian.

THE time has come that we have longed for; what greater or better work can be found than to proclaim the might of our Risen Lord? Bursting open the doors of the grave, He has displayed to us the glorious banner of His Resurrection. Through Him the sons of light are born to life eternal; the courts of the kingdom of heaven are opened to believers; and by the law of a blessed intercourse, earthly and heavenly things are interchanged. For by the Cross of Christ we have all been redeemed from death, and by His Resurrection the life of us all has risen again. While He has assumed our mortal nature, we acknowledge Him as the God of majesty; and in the glory of the Godhead we confess Him God and Man: Who by dying destroyed our death, and by rising again restored our life,—even Jesus Christ our Lord[y].

O GOD[z], Who by Thine Only-begotten Son hast overcome death, and opened unto us the gate of everlasting life; grant us, we beseech Thee, that we who celebrate the solemnities of our Lord's Resurrection, may by the renewing of Thy Spirit arise from the death of the soul; through the same Jesus Christ our Lord[a].

[y] Gelasian,—from two Easter Prefaces.
[z] This Collect supplies the introduction to our Gregorian Collect for Easter Day. This introduction is also prefixed to another Gelasian Collect, which prays, "Erige ad Te Tuorum corda credentium;" and to others in the Gothic Missal. See Muratori, i. 582; ii. 599, 604.
[a] Gelasian.

O ALMIGHTY God, hear Thy people, who are this day met to glorify the Resurrection of Thy Son our Lord; and guide them on from this festival to eternal gladness, from the exulting joy of this solemnity to joys that have no end. For this is the day of man's Resurrection, the birthday of eternal life; in which we have been satisfied with Thy mercy in the morning, in which the Blessed One Who cometh in the Name of the Lord, and Who is our God, hath shone upon us[b].

WE beseech Thee, O Lord, to preserve with watchful love those whom Thou hast cleansed; that those who have been redeemed by Thy Passion may rejoice in Thy Resurrection[c].

O GOD, Who hast appointed the Paschal Sacrifice for the world's salvation, be propitious to our supplications, that our supreme High Priest, interceding for us, may reconcile us, in that He is like unto us, and absolve us, in that He is equal to Thee, even Jesus Christ our Lord, Who with Thee, &c.[d]

O GOD, Who hast bestowed upon us the Paschal remedy, let Thy heavenly gift accompany Thy people; that what is now the cause of their delight in time, may hereafter be their joy throughout eternity; through Jesus Christ our Lord[e].

[b] Gothic Missal. [c] Gelasian. [d] Ibid. [e] Ibid.

BLOT out, we beseech Thee, O Lord, the handwriting made by the law of sin, which Thou hast made void in us by the Paschal mystery, through the Resurrection of Thy Son; through the same Jesus Christ our Lord[f].

WE beseech Thee, O Lord, be pleased by the Paschal remedies to grant unto us that we may learn to scorn earthly desires, and to long after things heavenly; through Jesus Christ our Lord[g].

GRANT, O merciful God, that in the Resurrection of our Lord Jesus Christ we may in very deed have our portion; through the same our Lord[h].

GRANT, we beseech Thee, Almighty God, that we who celebrate the Paschal solemnities may evermore live in Thy sanctifying grace; through Jesus Christ our Lord[i].

O GOD, Who by the Paschal solemnity hast bestowed healing gifts on the world, let Thy heavenly bounty attend Thy people, that they may both attain to perfect freedom, and advance to everlasting life; through Jesus Christ our Lord[k].

ALMIGHTY and everlasting God, Who hast vouchsafed the Paschal mystery in the covenant of man's reconciliation; grant unto our souls, that

[f] Gelasian. [g] Ibid. [h] Ibid. [i] Gregorian. [k] Ibid.

what we celebrate by our profession we may imitate in our practice; through Jesus Christ our Lord[l].

O GOD, Who by Christ's Resurrection restorest us to life eternal; raise us up to the Author of our salvation, Who is seated at Thy right hand; that He Who came to be judged for our sake, may come to judge in our favour, Jesus Christ Thy Son our Lord, Who with Thee, &c.[m]

GRANT, we beseech Thee, Almighty God, that we, putting off the old man with his deeds, may live according to His life, of Whose very self Thou hast made us partakers[n] by the healing gifts of Easter, Who with Thee, &c.[o]

O GOD, Who art the Author of our freedom and of our salvation, hear the voices of Thy suppliants, and grant that those whom Thou hast redeemed by the effusion of Thy Blood may both live by Thee, and enjoy perpetual safety in Thee, O Saviour of the world[p].

GRANT to us, O Lord, we beseech Thee, that as we celebrate the mysteries of the Resurrection of our Lord Jesus, so at His coming we may be enabled to rejoice with all His Saints; through the same Jesus Christ our Lord[q].

[l] Gregorian. [m] Ibid.
[n] Literally, "into Whose substance Thou hast transferred us."
[o] Gregorian. [p] Gothic. [q] Old Gallican.

LAMB of God, Who takest away the sin of the world, look upon us and have mercy upon us; Thou Who art Thyself both Victim and Priest, Thyself both Reward and Redeemer; keep safe from all evils those whom Thou hast redeemed, O Saviour of the world[r].

WE give Thee thanks, O God the Father, Who hast delivered us from the power of darkness, and translated us into the kingdom of Thy Son; grant therefore, we pray Thee, that as by His death He has recalled us to life, He may raise us up in His love to joys eternal[s].

ONLY-BEGOTTEN Son of God, Who didst willingly shed Thy Blood for us, whereby Thou reconciledst earth and heaven; grant us so to venerate the mystery of our redemption and Thy Resurrection, that we may be enabled to live perpetually in that peace which Thou Thyself art[t].

O GOD the Father Almighty, Who didst love the world with so great a love, that Thou willedst Thine Only-begotten Son to be crucified for its redemption; make us, who are redeemed with His precious Blood, to be so fruitful in works of love, that we may have our part in the first Resurrection, and not fear the power of the second death[u].

[r] Old Gallican. [s] Mozarabic. [t] Ibid. [u] Ibid.

ALMIGHTY God and Father, Who hast redeemed us with the precious Blood of Thy Son our Lord Jesus Christ, suffer not those who believe in Thee to be plunged into the abyss of eternal punishment; but grant that by confessing our sins we may be admitted into Thy presence, by Him on Whom Thou hast laid the iniquity of us all; that as we have been healed by His stripes, we may be defended by His unceasing protection [x].

WE confess, O Lord Jesus, that Thou hast died unto sin which was not Thine, but ours; and therefore, because having once died for the ungodly, Thou livest unto God, make us so to die unto sin once, that rising again to receive our crown, we may ever rejoice in Thine eternal gifts [y].

GRANT, we beseech Thee, Almighty God, that we who have gone through the Paschal festival, may by Thy bounty still keep it in our conduct and life; through Jesus Christ our Lord [z].

Ascension.

BE present, O Lord, to our supplications; that as we trust that the Saviour of mankind is seated with Thee in Thy Majesty, so we may feel that, according to His promise, He abideth with us unto the end of the world; through the same Jesus Christ our Lord [a].

[x] Mozarabic. [y] Ibid. [z] Gregorian. [a] Leonine.

ALMIGHTY and everlasting God, vouchsafe unto us, by the gift of this day's festival, that the aims of Thy children may thither be directed, where our substance, in Thine Only-begotten Son, is with Thee; through the same Jesus Christ our Lord[b].

HEAR us, O merciful God, and grant our minds to be lifted up, whither our Redeemer hath ascended; that at the second coming of the Mediator we may receive from Thy manifested bounty what we now venture to hope for as a promised gift; through the same Jesus Christ our Lord[c].

GRANT, we beseech Thee, Almighty God, that the faithful members of Thy Son may thither follow, whither our Head and Chief has gone before, Who with Thee, &c.[d]

O GOD, Who, to show forth the wonders of Thy Majesty, didst after Thy Resurrection from the dead ascend this day into heaven, in the presence of Thine Apostles, grant us the aid of Thy loving-kindness; that according to Thy promise Thou mayest ever dwell with us on earth, and we with Thee in heaven; where with the Father, &c.[e]

O LORD, Who hast borne our weak flesh to be glorified with Thee in heavenly places, take away the foulness of our sins, and restore to us the

[b] Leonine. [c] Ibid. [d] Ibid. [e] Gelasian.

dignity of our first estate; that by believing in Thee we may be able thither to ascend, whither we now believe Thee to have really ascended [f].

SAVIOUR and Lord, Who, ascending into heaven, wast pleased to show Thyself in glory to the eyes of beholders, while Thou didst promise to come as our Judge in like manner as Thou hadst ascended; make us to welcome this feast-day of Thine Ascension with pure and devout hearts; that we may in such wise ascend continually in Thee to a better life, that when Thou comest to the judgment, we may see Thy face and not be confounded [g].

O GOD, Who hast gone up on high, leading captivity captive, bestow on men the gifts of eternal peace: and as by ascending into heaven Thou hast withdrawn Thyself corporeally from human eyesight, be Thou graciously pleased to enter into our hearts [h].

Whitsuntide.

GRANT, we beseech Thee, Almighty God, that the splendour of Thy brightness may shine upon us, and the light of Thy Light confirm with the illumination of the Holy Spirit the hearts of those who have been born again through Thy grace: for the sake of Jesus Christ our Lord [i].

[f] Mozarabic. [g] Ibid. [h] Ibid. [i] Gregorian. Whitsun Eve.

GRANT, we beseech Thee, Almighty God, that we who celebrate the solemnity of the gift of the Holy Ghost, may be kindled with heavenly desires, and thirst for the fountain of life; through Jesus Christ our Lord[k].

ALMIGHTY and everlasting God, Who in the fulness of this day's mystery hast completed the secret work of the Paschal solemnity; grant, we beseech Thee, that we who have been made Thine adopted sons may obtain that peace which our Lord Jesus Christ left unto us when He came to Thee; through the same Jesus Christ our Lord[l].

WE beseech Thee, O Lord, let the Holy Spirit prepare our minds by Divine mysteries, forasmuch as He Himself is the remission of all sins; through Jesus Christ our Lord[m].

WE beseech Thee, O Lord, let the power of the Holy Spirit be present with us, that it may both mercifully cleanse our hearts, and protect us from all adversities; through our Lord Jesus Christ[n].

O GOD, Who by the mystery of this day's festival dost sanctify Thy universal Church in every race and nation, shed abroad throughout the whole world the gift of the Holy Spirit; that the work wrought

[k] Gregorian, Whitsun Eve. [l] Leonine. [m] Ibid. [n] Ibid.

by Divine goodness at the first preaching of the Gospel may now also be extended among believing hearts; through Jesus Christ our Lord[o].

O GOD, Who wast pleased to send on Thy disciples the Holy Spirit, the Paraclete, in the burning fire of Thy love, grant to Thy people to be fervent in the unity of faith; that evermore abiding in Thee, they may be found both stedfast in faith and active in work; through Jesus Christ our Lord[p].

MAY the Spirit, the Paraclete, O Lord, Who proceedeth from Thee, illuminate our minds, and, as Thy Son hath promised, lead us into all truth; through the same our Lord Jesus Christ[q].

MAY the outpouring of the Holy Spirit, O Lord, cleanse our hearts, and make them fruitful with its plenteous dew; through our Lord Jesus Christ[r].

O GOD, Who gavest the Holy Spirit to Thine Apostles, vouchsafe a good effect to Thy people's devout prayer; that as Thou hast given them faith, Thou mayest also bestow on them peace, through Jesus Christ our Lord[s].

WE beseech Thee, O Lord, let the Holy Spirit enkindle in us that fire which our Lord

[o] Gelasian. [p] Ibid. [q] Ibid. [r] Ibid. [s] Gregorian.

Jesus Christ sent upon the earth, and ardently desired to see enkindled[t], Who with Thee, &c.[u]

O GOD, the Enlightener and the Life of believers, the ineffable greatness of Whose gifts is celebrated by the testimony of this day's festival; grant unto Thy people to apprehend in their understandings what they have learned by a miracle, that Thine adopted children, whom the Holy Spirit has called together, may love Thee without any lukewarmness, and confess Thy faith without any dissension; through Jesus Christ our Lord[x].

WE beseech Thine Omnipotence, Holy God, Father Almighty, that Thou wouldest fill us with the gift of Thine Only-begotten Son, and the ineffable blessing, visitation, and life-giving power of Thine and His Holy Spirit; whereby Thy Church, enkindled with His fire, may hold the true faith in Him from Whom she receives all truth[y].

LET Thy mercy, O Lord, be upon us, and the brightness of Thy Spirit illumine our inward souls; that He may kindle our cold hearts and light up our dark minds, Who abideth evermore with Thee in glory[z].

[t] According to one interpretation (perhaps not the most satisfactory one) of Luke xii. 49.
[u] Gregorian.
[x] Gothic, and partly Leonine.
[y] Mozarabic.
[z] Ibid.

O HOLY Spirit, Who proceedest from the Father and the Son, teach us to do the truth, that Thou mayest unite us in a mysterious bond of love to the Father and Son, from Whom Thou proceedest so ineffably [a].

LET Thy Spirit, O Lord, come into the midst of us, and washing us with the pure water of repentance, prepare us to be alway a living sacrifice unto Thee [b].

HEAVENLY King, Paraclete, Spirit of Truth, Who art everywhere present and fillest all things, the Treasury of good things and the Bestower of life, come and dwell in us, and purify us from every stain, and save our souls, in Thy goodness [c].

Trinity Sunday.

O LORD God, Father Almighty, bless and protect, through Thine Only Son, in the power of the Holy Spirit, Thy servants who are obedient to Thy majesty; that being free from fear of all enemies, they may continually rejoice in praising Thee; through the same Jesus Christ our Lord [d].

[a] Mozarabic. [b] Ibid.
[c] Midnight Office of Eastern Church.
[d] From a Missa appended to the Gregorian. The Collect for this service is our Collect for Trinity Sunday. Menard places this Missa in the Sacramentary itself.

LORD Jesus Christ, pour into us the Holy Spirit promised by the Father, that He may give us life, and teach us the fulness of truth in the Mystery of the blessed and undivided Trinity; that our salvation may be perfectly accomplished by His gift, wherein consists the perfection of all virtue [e].

O HOLY Spirit the Comforter, Who with the Father and the Son abidest One God in Trinity; descend this day into our hearts, that while Thou makest intercession for us, we may with full confidence call upon our Father [f].

MAY the infinite and ineffable Trinity, the Father, the Son, and the Holy Ghost, direct our life in good works, and after our passage through this world vouchsafe to us eternal rest with the righteous. Grant this, O Eternal and Almighty God [g].

O LORD, the Saviour and Guardian of such as fear Thee, turn away from Thy Church the deceitful allurements of this world's wisdom; that under the teaching of Thy Spirit, we may find pleasure in the prophetic delineations and the apo-

[e] Mozarabic. Of these Mozarabic prayers, the first two are prescribed for Whitsunday (Brev. 422, Miss. 263), the third for the Sunday following (Brev. 423).

[f] Ibid.

[g] Ibid.

stolic instructions, rather than in the terms of philosophy; lest the vanity of falsehoods should deceive those whom the teaching of truth illuminates; through Jesus Christ our Lord[h].

BLESSED and glorious Trinity, Father, Son, and Holy Spirit, thanks be to Thee, very and one Trinity, one and perfect Godhead. Thee, God the Father Unbegotten; Thee, the Only-begotten Son; Thee, the Holy Spirit the Paraclete; the Holy and Undivided Trinity, do we confess and praise with heart and mouth; to Thee be glory for ever, Alleluia[i].

Saints' Days.

O GOD, the Strength of all Thy Saints, Who hast granted them in Thine abundant bounty the grace to come to their present glory; vouchsafe, we beseech Thee, pardon to our sins, that we may be able worthily to celebrate their solemnities; through Jesus Christ our Lord[k].

O LORD our God, multiply upon us Thy grace, and grant us to follow, by a holy profession,

[h] Gelasian. *In Dominica Octavorum Pentecosten.* This Sunday was not dedicated to the mystery of the Holy Trinity by any general authority in the Western Church until the fourteenth century. But Martene (iii. 548) refers to very old service-books which had for this day a preface, a benediction, or a whole Mass, dwelling on that mystery; to which, indeed, the thoughts of Whitsuntide would naturally conduct.

[i] Sarum Sunday Office, Anthems after Athanasian Creed.

[k] Leonine.

the triumph of those whose glorious conflicts we celebrate; through Jesus Christ our Lord[l].

GRANT, O Almighty God, that we may evermore praise Thee in the commemoration of Thy Saints; for Thou wilt be careful to cherish those whom Thou hast enabled to persevere in honouring Thee; through Jesus Christ our Lord[m].

ALMIGHTY and everlasting God, Who hast enabled Thy Saints not only to believe in Thy Son, but also to suffer for His sake; extend Thy Divine aid also to our weakness, that as they breathed out their happy souls for the hope of Thine everlasting mercy, we may at least attain it by a sincere confession of Thee; through Jesus Christ our Lord[n].

ALMIGHTY and everlasting God, Who adornest the sacred body of Thy Church by the confessions of holy Martyrs; grant us, we pray Thee, that both by their doctrines and their pious example, we may follow after what is pleasing in Thy sight; through Jesus Christ our Lord[o].

MERCIFULLY give us, O Lord, an increase of faith in Thee; that as it glorifies Thy holy Martyrs who held it fast even unto blood, it may

[l] Leonine. [m] Ibid. [n] Ibid. [o] Ibid.

also justify us who follow it in truth; through Jesus Christ our Lord [p].

GRANT, we beseech Thee, O Lord our God, that as we welcome with a temporary service the commemoration of Thy Saints, so we may rejoice in beholding them perpetually; through Jesus Christ our Lord [q].

GRANT, we beseech Thee, Almighty God, that the examples of Thy Saints may stir us up to a better life, so that we who celebrate their solemnities, may also imitate their actions; through Jesus Christ our Lord [r].

O GOD, Who permittest us to celebrate the commemoration of all Thy Saints, grant that we Thy servants may enjoy their fellowship in eternal gladness; through Jesus Christ our Lord [s].

ALMIGHTY and everlasting God, Who dost enkindle the flame of Thy love in the hearts of the Saints, grant to our minds the same faith and power of love; that as we rejoice in their triumphs, we may profit by their examples; through Jesus Christ our Lord [t].

[p] Leonine. [q] Ibid. [r] Gregorian.
[s] Annexed to Gregorian Sacram. From a *Missa Communis Sanctorum*, in what Muratori calls an "additamentum in calce codicis Othoboniani." [t] Gothic.

O GOD, Who hast enkindled in the holy bosoms of all Thy Saints so great an ardour of faith, that they despised all bodily pains, while hastening with all spiritual earnestness to Thee the Author of life; hear our prayers, and grant that the hateful sweetness of sin may wax faint in us, and we may glow with the infused warmth of love for Thee; through Thy mercy, &c. [w]

O CHRIST the Son of God, our great joy and everlasting gladness, Who after their bitter sufferings dost vouchsafe to Thy Saints the contemplation of Thy sweetness, so that pain and groaning have no more place among them; bestow now on us, though undeserving, the healing gift of comfort; that we who through our own fault have been far removed from Thee, may be gathered into the company of Thy Saints, and with them attain to infinite gladness; through Thy mercy, &c. [x]

During Trinity Time.

PRAYERS FOR VARIOUS GRACES.

1. *For Conversion of Will to God.*

ALMIGHTY and everlasting God, convert us with our whole souls to Thyself; that as Thou vouchsafest such good gifts to the undeserving,

[w] Mozarabic. [x] Ibid.

Thou mayest bestow yet greater on the devout; through Jesus Christ our Lord[y].

ALMIGHTY and everlasting God, convert our minds, we beseech Thee, to deeds which shall be pleasing in Thy sight; that Thy rebuke may not prove, by our neglect, a greater cause of punishment, but, by our amendment, a Fatherly admonition; through Jesus Christ our Lord[z].

WE beseech Thee, O Lord, convert all our hearts unto Thyself, that we, abstaining from things which offend Thee, may feel Thy mercy, and not Thy wrath; through Jesus Christ our Lord[a].

O ETERNAL Father, convert our hearts unto Thyself; for nothing needful shall be lacking to those whom Thou shalt enable to be devoted to Thy worship; through Jesus Christ our Lord[b].

WE beseech Thee, Almighty God, look not upon the multitude of our wickednesses; but draw away our weakness from sin, and guide the wills of Thy servants to what is right; through Jesus Christ our Lord[c].

O LORD our God, Whose compassion is the first cause of our fearing and loving Thy

[y] Leonine. [z] Ibid. [a] Ibid. [b] Ibid. [c] Ibid.

Name, mercifully pour (Thy grace) into our hearts, that we, casting away what displeases Thee, may be united to Thee with an honest will; through Jesus Christ our Lord [d].

O GOD, the Comforter of the humble, and the Strength of the faithful, be merciful to Thy suppliants; that human weakness, which by itself is prone to fall, may be evermore supported by Thee to stand upright; through Jesus Christ our Lord [e].

O GOD, the Bestower of peace and the Lover of charity, grant to Thy servants a true agreement with Thy will, that we may be delivered from all the temptations which attack us; through Jesus Christ our Lord [f].

THOU hast healed our wounds, O Lord, by the wounds of Thine Only-begotten Son. What then shall we do now that we have been bought with so great a price? how shall we serve such a Lord, by Whom liberty is promised and an inheritance is offered to us? Work in us, O Lord, what may please Thee; that we may possess Thee, do Thou possess us. We will not go back from Thee; Thou wilt let us live, and we will call upon Thy Name [g].

[d] Leonine. [e] Gelasian. [f] Ibid. [g] Mozarabic.

2. For the Fear of God.

DELIVER us from evil, and confirm us in Thy fear and in good works, O Trinity, our God, Who art blessed, and dost live, and govern all things, world without end[h].

O GOD, Who by the prophet's voice dost pronounce those blessed that fear Thee; grant us to render an acceptable obedience in Thy fear, and make us henceforth to walk in Thy ways; and let our work under Thy direction be pleasing in Thy sight, and its fruit be sweet in the day of reward[i].

3. For Humility.

ALMIGHTY and everlasting God, Who resistest the proud, and givest grace to the humble; grant, we beseech Thee, that we may not exalt ourselves and provoke Thine indignation, but bow down and receive the gifts of Thy mercy; through Jesus Christ our Lord[k].

O GOD, by Whose will all things were made, and by Whose truth they continue in being; we beseech Thee to keep us under Thy shelter, lest we be cast down from our chief happiness by the swellings of pride; grant us ever to ascend into heaven by the steps of humility; and because Thou art the Fountain of life, from Thee may we

[h] Mozarabic. [i] Ibid. [k] Leonine.

drink what by faith we thirst for; in Thy light may we shine with the light of knowledge, and reap the fruit of righteousness in an everlasting exaltation [l].

O GOD, Who art rich in forgiveness, and for this cause willedst to assume our lowly flesh, that Thou mightest leave to us an example of humility, and make us stedfast in all manner of sufferings; grant that we may always hold fast the good things which we receive from Thee, and as often as we fall into sins, may be raised up by repentance; through Thy mercy [m].

4. *For Faith.*

WE beseech Thee, O Lord, in Thy compassion to increase Thy faith in us; because Thou wilt not deny the aid of Thy loving-kindness to those on whom Thou bestowest a stedfast belief in Thee; through Jesus Christ our Lord [n].

GRANT us, O Lord, we pray Thee, to trust in Thee with all our heart; seeing that as Thou dost alway resist the proud who confide in their own strength, so Thou dost not forsake those who make their boast of Thy mercy; through Jesus Christ our Lord [o].

[l] Mozarabic.
[m] Gothic Missal.
[n] Leonine.
[o] Ibid.

CONFIRM, O Lord, in our minds the mysteries of the true faith, that as we confess Him Who was conceived by the Virgin to be Very God and Man, so by the power of His saving Resurrection we may be enabled to attain eternal joy; through the same Jesus Christ our Lord[p].

BE gracious to our prayers, O merciful God, and guard Thy people with loving protection; that they who confess Thine Only-begotten Son as God born in our bodily flesh, may never be corrupted by the deceits of the devil; through the same Jesus Christ our Lord[q].

O GOD, Who art One and True, we humbly beseech Thee that the Catholic Faith, which is acceptable to Thee, may continue for ever in us all; through Jesus Christ our Lord[r].

LORD Jesus Christ, Very God and Very Man, Who changest not, but art holy in all Thy works; turn away from us the unbelief of a doubtful mind, and fill our heart with the gifts of Thy grace; that we may believe and know Thee to be Very God, Who by miracles and mighty works art proved to be the Saviour of all[s].

WE beseech Thee, O Lord, continually to strengthen us by a sincere faith in Thine

[p] Gregorian. [q] Ambrosian. [r] Gallican Missal. [s] Mozarabic.

Incarnation; that the crafty enemy may never be able to overcome us who are established in the love of Thee[t].

ARISE, O Lord, Who judgest the earth; and as Thou dwellest in and possessest the faith of all nations, suffer us not to abide in darkness; and grant that we may not lay the foundations of our faith on the sand where the whirlwind may overthrow them, but be established on the rock which is stedfast in Thee[u].

5. *For Hope.*

IT is good for us to hold fast by Thee, O Lord; but do Thou so increase in us the desire of good, that the hope which joins us to Thee may not be shaken by any wavering of faith, but may endure in stedfastness of love[x].

MAY the hope which Thou hast given us, O Lord, be our consolation in our low estate, as it will fill us with glory in the day of our rejoicing[y].

MERCIFUL Lord, the Comforter and Teacher of Thy faithful people, increase in Thy Church the desires which Thou hast given, and confirm the hearts of those who hope in Thee by enabling them

[t] Mozarabic. [u] Ibid. [x] Ibid. [y] Ibid.

to understand the depth of Thy promises; that all Thine adopted sons may even now behold with the eyes of faith, and patiently wait for, the light which as yet Thou dost not openly manifest; through Jesus Christ our Lord[a].

6. *For Love.*

O GOD, Who hast taught Thy Church to keep all Thy heavenly commandments by loving Thy Godhead and our neighbour; grant us the spirit of peace and grace, that Thy universal family may be both devoted to Thee with their whole heart, and united to each other with a pure will; through Jesus Christ our Lord[a].

CONFIRM, O Lord, we pray Thee, the hearts of Thy children, and strengthen them with the power of Thy grace; that they may both be devout in prayer to Thee, and sincere in love for each other; through Jesus Christ our Lord[b].

O GOD, Who makest all things profitable to them that love Thee, grant to our hearts an invincible power[c] of love, that the desires which have been conceived by Thine inspiration may not be changed by any temptation; through Jesus Christ our Lord[d].

[a] Ambrosian. [a] Leonine. [b] Ibid.
[c] *Effectum.* Perhaps it should be *affectum.* [d] Gelasian.

GIVE strength, O Lord, to those who seek Thee, and continually pour into their souls the holy desire of seeking Thee; that they who long to see Thy face may not crave the world's pernicious pleasure [e].

ABBA, Father, fulfil the office of Thy Name towards Thy servants; do Thou govern, protect, preserve, sanctify, guide, console them; let them be so enkindled with love for Thee, that they may not be despised by Thee, O most merciful Lord, most tender Father [f]!

7. *For Sacred Knowledge.*

SHOW the light of Thy countenance upon us, O Lord, that the going-forth of Thy word may give light and understanding, to nourish the hearts of the simple; and that while our desire is set on Thy commandments, we may receive with open heart the Spirit of wisdom and understanding [g].

O GOD, with Whom is the well of life, and in Whose light we see light; increase in us, we beseech Thee, the brightness of Divine knowledge, whereby we may be able to reach Thy plenteous fountain; impart to our thirsting souls the draught of life, and restore to our darkened minds the light from heaven [h].

[e] Mozarabic. [f] Gallican Sacramentary. [g] Mozarabic. [h] Ibid.

8. *For Heavenly Mindedness.*

ALMIGHTY and merciful God, unto Whose everlasting blessedness we ascend, not by the frailty of the flesh, but by the activity of the soul; make us ever, by Thine inspiration, to seek after the courts of the heavenly City, and, by Thy mercy, confidently to enter them; through Jesus Christ our Lord [i].

GRANT us, O Lord, not to mind earthly things, but to love things heavenly; and even now, while we are placed among things that are passing away, to cleave to those that shall abide; through Jesus Christ our Lord [k].

INCLINE our heart, O Lord, unto Thy testimonies, and turn it away from beholding vanity: that Thou mayest detach us from the love of earthly things, and unite our affection to things above [l].

9. *For Peace.*

O ETERNAL Son, Who abidest for ever, Consubstantial with the Father, equal to Him as enthroned and as Creator; Thou, without being changed, didst assume our flesh, and being made Man, like unto us in all but sin, wast made our Mediator with the Father. Thou hast broken down the partition wall, and hast reconciled the

[i] Leonine. [k] Ibid. [l] Mozarabic.

earthly with the heavenly, and made of twain one, by Thine Incarnation. Thou saidst to Thy holy Apostles and disciples, "My peace I give unto you;" grant us now that peace, O Lord[m].

O GOD of love, O Giver of concord, Who hast given one counsel for our profit, with a new commandment, through Thine Only-begotten Son, that we should love one another, even as Thou didst love us, the unworthy and the wandering, and gavest Thy beloved Son for our life and salvation; we pray Thee, Lord, give to us Thy servants, in all time of our life on the earth, (but especially and pre-eminently now,) a mind forgetful of past ill-will, a pure conscience and sincere thoughts, and a heart to love our brethren[n].

O GOD, Who art the unsearchable abyss of peace, the ineffable sea of love, the fountain of blessings, and the bestower of affection, Who sendest peace to those that receive it; open to us this day the sea of Thy love, and water us with plenteous streams from the riches of Thy grace, and from the most sweet springs of Thy benignity. Make us children of quietness, and heirs of peace. Enkindle in us the fire of Thy love; sow in us Thy fear; strengthen our weakness by Thy power;

[m] Coptic Liturgy of S. Gregory Theologus. All but one of these prayers are connected with the Eucharistic Kiss of Peace.
[n] Coptic Liturgy of S. Cyril.

bind us closely to Thee and to each other in one firm and indissoluble bond of unity [o].

O GOD the Father, Origin of Divinity, Good beyond all that is good, Fair beyond all that is fair, in Whom is calmness, peace, and concord; do Thou make up the dissensions which divide us from each other, and bring us back into an unity of love, which may bear some likeness to Thy sublime Nature. And as Thou art above all things, make us one by the unanimity of a good mind, that through the embrace of charity and the bonds of affection we may be spiritually one, as well in ourselves as in each other, through that peace of Thine which maketh all things peaceful, and through the grace, mercy, and tenderness of Thine Only-begotten Son [p].

WE beseech Thee, O Lord, to keep us in perpetual peace, as Thou hast vouchsafed us confidence in Thee; through Jesus Christ our Lord [q].

DISPOSE our days in Thy peace, and command us to be rescued from eternal condemnation, and numbered in the flock of Thine elect [r].

[o] Syrian Clementine Liturgy.
[p] Jacobite Liturgy of S. Dionysius. [q] Gelasian.
[r] Gregorian. These words, Bede tells us, ii. 1, were added by Gregory to the Eucharistic Canon.

O CHRIST, the Word of the Most High Father, Who wast made Flesh to dwell among us, enter into our hearts, that all we who have been redeemed by the mystery of Thine Incarnation, may remain united in the fellowship of perpetual peace [s].

LORD God Almighty, Christ the King of glory, Who art our true Peace, and Love eternal; enlighten our souls with the brightness of Thy peace, and purify our consciences with the sweetness of Thy love, that we may with peaceful hearts wait for the Author of peace, and in the adversities of this world may ever have Thee for our Guardian and Protector; and so being fenced about by Thy care, may heartily give ourselves to the love of Thy peace [t].

O GOD, Who of Thy great love to this world, didst reconcile earth to heaven through Thine Only-begotten Son; grant that we who, by the darkness of our sins, are turned aside from brotherly love, may by Thy light shed forth in our souls be filled with Thine own sweetness, and embrace our friends in Thee, and our enemies for Thy sake, in a bond of mutual affection [u].

O GOD, Who art Peace everlasting, Whose chosen reward is the gift of peace, and Who

[s] Mozarabic. [t] Ibid. [u] Ibid.

hast taught us that the peace-makers are Thy children, pour Thy sweet peace into our souls, that everything discordant may utterly vanish, and all that makes for peace be sweet to us for ever[x].

10. *For Deliverance from Temptation.*

ALMIGHTY and everlasting God, mercifully grant unto Thy Church, that deadly pleasures may be cast aside, and that it may rather rejoice in the gladness of Thine eternal salvation; through Jesus Christ our Lord[y].

WE beseech Thee, O Lord, to renew Thy people inwardly and outwardly, that as Thou wouldest not have them to be hindered by bodily pleasures, Thou mayest make them vigorous with spiritual purpose; and refresh them in such sort by things transitory, that Thou mayest grant them rather to cleave to things eternal; through Jesus Christ our Lord[z].

PROTECT, O Lord, Thy suppliants, support their weakness, and wash away their earthly stains; and while they walk amid the darkness of this mortal life, do Thou ever quicken them by Thy light; deliver them in Thy mercy from all evils, and grant them to attain the height of good: through Jesus Christ our Lord[a].

[x] Mozarabic. [y] Leonine. [z] Ibid. [a] Ibid.

IN Thy mercy and majesty, O Lord, behold Thy household, that they may be neither stained with vices of their own, nor held in bondage by the sins of others; but that being ever freed and cleansed from both, they may do service unto Thee; through Jesus Christ our Lord [b].

HEAR us, O Lord our God, and separate the hearts of Thy faithful people from the wickedness of the world; that they who call Thee Lord with their own voice may not fall back into the service of the devil; through Jesus Christ our Lord [c].

GRANT, we beseech Thee, Almighty God, that pressing onwards in Thy way with devout minds, we may escape the snares of the sins that beset us; through Jesus Christ our Lord [d].

WE pray Thee, O Lord, be present to Thy suppliants; and amid the snares of a wicked world, protect our weakness with never-failing love; through Jesus Christ our Lord [e].

O GOD, Who didst mitigate the flames of fire for the Three Children; grant, we beseech Thee, that we Thy servants may not be burned by the flame of sins, through Jesus Christ our Lord [f].

[b] Leonine. [c] Ibid. [d] Ibid. [e] Gelasian. [f] Ibid.

O GOD, Who dwellest in the holy, and forsakest not pious hearts, deliver us from earthly desires and carnal appetites; that no sin may reign in us, but that we may with free spirits serve Thee, our only Lord; through Jesus Christ[g].

11. *For Purity.*

POUR out, O Lord, we beseech Thee, the Spirit of grace upon Thy family, and cast out from them whatever evil they have incurred by the fraud of the devil or by earthly corruption; that being cleansed within and without, they may ever render unto Thee a pure worship, and may the more readily obtain what they fitly and reasonably ask; through Jesus Christ our Lord[h].

WE beseech Thee, O Lord, be gracious to Thy people, that they, abhorring day by day the things which displease Thee, may be more and more filled with the love of Thy commandments, and being supported by Thy comfort in this mortal life, may advance to the full enjoyment of life immortal; through Jesus Christ our Lord[i].

MAKE us, O Lord, to flourish like pure lilies in the courts of Thine house, and to show forth to the faithful the fragrance of good works and the example of a godly life, through Thy mercy, &c.[k]

[g] Gelasian. [h] Leonine. [i] Ibid. [k] Mozarabic.

O GOD, Who ever lovest what is true, and bringest to light what is hidden, Who wast pleased to come into the Virgin's womb for the world's salvation; sprinkle us with the hyssop of Thy word, and purify us from our iniquities; and mercifully pour into our souls a right spirit to call upon Thee; through Thy mercy, &c.[l]

12. *For Guidance.*

MERCIFULLY regard, O Lord, the prayers of Thy family, and while they submit themselves to Thee with their whole heart, do Thou prosper, support, encompass them; that relying on Thee as their Guide, they may be entangled in no evils, and replenished with all good; through Jesus Christ our Lord[m].

WE beseech Thee, O Lord, in Thy loving-kindness, set in order our life and conversation, that no adversities may prevail against us, and nothing salutary be wanting to us, through Jesus Christ our Lord[n].

O GOD, the Author and Giver of true blessedness, guide us into the path of the undefiled; that seeking the testimonies of Thy law with pious hearts, we may continually love what Thou com-

[l] Mozarabic. [m] Leonine. [n] Ibid.

mandest, and desire that whereunto they lead; through Jesus Christ our Lord[o].

MAKE us, we beseech Thee, O Lord, obedient to Thy commandments, for then shall all things go prosperously with us, if we follow the Author of our whole life; through Jesus Christ our Lord[p].

GRANT to Thy servants, O Lord, the pardon of their sins, comfort in life, and perpetual guidance; whereby they may faithfully serve Thee, and be alway enabled to attain Thy mercy; through Jesus Christ our Lord[q].

JESU our Master, do Thou meet us while we walk in the way, and long to reach the Country[r]; so that following Thy light, we may keep the way of righteousness, and never wander away into the horrible darkness of this world's night, while Thou, Who art the Way, the Truth, and the Life, art shining within us[s].

O LORD, our support and our refuge, deliver us from temptation, give us the defence of Thy salvation, hold us up with Thy right hand, teach us

[o] Gelasian. [p] Ibid. [q] Ibid.

[r] The well-known antithesis between *via*, the pilgrim's path in this world, which is the region of faith, and *patria*, the heavenly country, which is the region of fruition. Compare the words "Quod sum causa Tuæ viæ," i.e. "of Thy walk through this world," and the "O bona patria," the "dear, dear country," of Bernard de Morlaix.

[s] Mozarabic.

by Thy discipline, and make our way and our life undefiled [t].

GUIDE us in Thy way, O Christ, and mercifully show the fountain of wisdom to our thirsting minds; that we may be free from sorrowful heaviness, and may drink in the sweetness of life eternal [u].

BE Thou, O Lord, our protection, Who art our redemption; direct our minds by Thy gracious presence, and watch over our paths with guiding love; that among the snares which lie hidden in this path wherein we walk, we may so pass onward with hearts fixed on Thee, that by the track of faith we may come to be where Thou wouldest have us [x].

13. *For Contentment.*

GRANT, O Lord, that Thy family, devoted to Thy service, and confiding in Thy protection, may obtain the blessing which they humbly implore; that being at rest under Thy defence, they may not be left destitute of assistance for this life, and may be prepared for the good things which are eternal; through Jesus Christ our Lord [y].

BE present, O Lord, to Thy suppliants, and graciously protect those who place their whole trust in Thy mercy; that being cleansed from the

[t] Mozarabic. [u] Ibid. [x] Ibid. [y] Leonine.

stain of sin, they may continue in holy living, and being sufficiently supplied with temporal blessings, may attain the inheritance of Thy promises; through Jesus Christ our Lord[a].

GRANT us, O Lord, we beseech Thee, always to seek Thy kingdom and righteousness; and of whatsoever Thou seest us to stand in need, mercifully grant us an abundant portion; through Jesus Christ our Lord[a].

O GOD, Who hast forbidden us[b] to be anxious about supplies for this life; grant, we beseech Thee, that we may devotedly follow after what belongeth to Thee, and that all things salutary may be granted to us; through Jesus Christ our Lord[c].

14. *For Spiritual Joy.*

LET Thy perpetual mercy, O Lord, accompany Thy Church; that while it is placed among the storms of the world, it may both be refreshed with present gladness, and behold the brightness of eternal bliss; through Jesus Christ our Lord[d].

GRANT us, we beseech Thee, O Lord our God, ever to rejoice in devotion to Thee; because our happiness is perpetual and full, if we are con-

[a] Leonine. [a] Gelasian.
[b] The text has *voluisti*, which is obviously a mistake for *noluisti*. Murat. i. 605.
[c] Gelasian. [d] Leonine.

tinually serving the Author of all good; through Jesus Christ our Lord[e].

WE beseech Thee, O Lord, let Thy faithful people rejoice evermore in Thy benefits; that being ordered by Thy governance, they may please Thee in their lives, and happily obtain the good which they pray for; through Jesus Christ our Lord[f].

GRANT, O Almighty God, that we may attain to the fulness of joy, and be the more earnestly devoted to Thy Majesty; through Jesus Christ our Lord[g].

LORD, pour into the hearts of Thy servants that joy of the righteous which is in Thee; that the praise of Thee, which becometh well the upright, may purge out all unholiness from our minds; through Thy mercy, &c.[h]

15. *For Thankfulness*[i].

O GOD, Who chastisest us in Thy love, and refreshest us amid Thy chastening; grant that we may ever be able to give Thee thanks for both; through Jesus Christ our Lord[k].

WE beseech Thee, Almighty God, that the prosperity bestowed upon us may not lead us

[e] Leonine. [f] Ibid. [g] Ibid. [h] Mozarabic.
[i] See below, "Thanksgiving on Removal of Calamities." [k] Leonine.

to be ashamed of Thy worship, but rather may alway enkindle us to render heartier thanks to Thee; through Jesus Christ our Lord[l].

16. *For Recovery of Lost Happiness.*

GRANT, O merciful God, that we who by violating the Divine precepts fell away from the happiness of Paradise, may by the keeping of Thy commandments regain the access to eternal bliss; through Jesus Christ our Lord[m].

17. *For Angelic Ministrations.*

O GOD, Who orderest things in heaven and earth alike for the assistance of mankind; we beseech Thee that while we are labouring in the lower part of the universe, Thou wouldest mercifully refresh us by the protection of Thy ministers from above; through Jesus Christ our Lord[n].

O LIGHT of light, O Brightness indescribable, Christ our God, the Wisdom, Power, and Glory of the Father, Who didst appear visibly to all men as the Word made flesh, and having overcome the prince of darkness, didst return to Thy throne on high; grant to us Thy suppliants, amid this dark world, the full outpouring of Thy splendour; appoint the Archangel Michael to be our defender, to guard our going out and coming in; and admit

[l] Leonine. [m] Ibid. [n] Ibid.

us to a place on Thy right hand, to receive the crown from Thee [o].

18. *For Perseverance.*

O GOD, Who in Thy loving-kindness dost both begin and finish all good things [p]; grant that as we glory in the beginnings of Thy grace, so we may rejoice in its completion; through Jesus Christ our Lord [q].

ALMIGHTY and everlasting God, Whose paths are alway mercy and truth, grant, we beseech Thee, that we who are fostered by Thy tenderness may also grow up with an increase of piety; through Jesus Christ our Lord [r].

O GOD, Who hast willed that the gate of mercy should stand open to the faithful; look on us, and have mercy upon us; that we who by Thy grace are following the path of Thy will, may never turn aside from the ways of life; through Jesus Christ our Lord [s].

O GOD, Who bestowest this upon us by Thy grace, that we should be made righteous instead of ungodly, blessed instead of miserable; be present to Thine own works, be present to Thine own gifts; that they in whom dwells a justifying faith

[o] Mozarabic. [p] See Phil. i. 6. [q] Leonine.
[r] Leonine. [s] Gelasian.

may not lack a strong perseverance; through Jesus Christ our Lord[t].

LOOK upon us and hear us, O Lord our God; and assist those endeavours to please Thee which Thou Thyself hast granted to us; as Thou hast given the first act of will, so give the completion of the work; grant that we may be able to finish what Thou hast granted us to wish to begin[u].

HEAR my prayer, O Lord, and let my cry come up to the ears of Thy gracious mercy; do not cut us off in the midst of our days, but grant us, as those who make for a well-known goal, to finish our course of holy living; and by a hearty pursuit of sanctification in the few days of our present life, to win the eternal kingdom of glory[x].

GRANT Thy servants, O God, to be set on fire with Thy Spirit, strengthened by Thy power, illuminated by Thy splendour, filled with Thy grace, and to go forward by Thine aid. Give them, O Lord, a right faith, perfect love, true humility. Grant, O Lord, that there may be in us simple affection, brave patience, persevering obedience, perpetual peace, a pure mind, a right and clean heart, a good will, a holy conscience, spiritual com-

[t] Old Gallican Missal. [u] Mozarabic. [x] Ibid.

punction, ghostly strength, a life unspotted and unblameable; and after having manfully finished our course, may we be enabled happily to enter into Thy kingdom [y].

10. *For a Happy Death.*

O GOD, Who art the Saviour of all the living, Who willest not the death of sinners, nor rejoicest in the perdition of those that die, I humbly entreat Thee to vouchsafe me pardon of my offences, that I may bewail what I have committed, and henceforth commit them no more; and that when my last day and the end of my life has arrived, Thy holy Angel may receive me cleansed from all offences; through Jesus Christ our Lord [z].

O GOD of love and peace, Who for the salvation of mankind didst endure to be hanged on a Cross, and didst pour forth Thy Blood for our redemption; favourably and benignantly receive my prayers, and bestow on me Thy mercy; that when Thou shalt command me to depart from the body, the enemy may have no power over me, but the Angel of peace may place me among Thy Saints and elect, where light abides and life reigns, world without end [a].

[y] Gallican Sacramentary. [z] Ibid. It occurs also in a *Missa propria Sacerdotis* in an appendix to Muratori's edition of the Gregorian Sacramentary. Mur. ii. 385. [a] Ibid.

20. *For Mercy in the Judgment.*

DELIVER me, O Lord, from eternal death, in that tremendous day when the heavens and the earth shall be shaken, when Thou shalt come to judge the world by fire. That day is a day of wrath, of calamity and misery, a great day and very bitter. What shall I, most wretched, say or do, when I have no good thing to bring before the awful Judge? Now, O Christ, we appeal to Thee —we pray Thee, pity us: Thou Who camest to redeem the lost, condemn not Thou the redeemed[b].

IN that time of terror and of dread, that time full of sadness, have pity, O Lord, on those who confess Thy Passion. Have Thou a care of those who put their trust in Thy love for men, and do Thou forgive their sins. Let Thy tenderness be stirred up for those who invoke Thy holy Name; nor let Thy grace fail us. Rebuke not the ministers of Thy kingdom for their filthy raiment. Let not the light of our lamps be put out. Let not Thy justice be against us. Show the aid of Thy grace against our wickedness. Pour out the flood of Thy pity on our ungodliness, and wash away our sins, and efface in us whatever is hateful. Give us true and uncorrupt faith, a pure and tranquil life,

[b] Sarum Office of the Dead.

high and holy gifts, freedom from severe temptations, a departure with due preparation, a good end, richest blessings, lasting delights, inheritance with the Saints, and confidence when we stand before Thine awful throne, because Thou art merciful and rich in bounty [c].

21. *A General Prayer.*

GIVE me, O Lord, purity of lips, a clean and innocent heart, and rectitude of action. Give me humility, patience, abstinence, chastity, prudence, justice, fortitude, temperance. Give me the Spirit of wisdom and understanding, the Spirit of counsel and strength, the Spirit of knowledge and godliness, and of Thy fear. Make me ever to seek Thy face with all my heart, all my soul, all my mind; grant me to have a contrite and humbled heart in Thy presence—to prefer nothing to Thy love. Most high, eternal, and ineffable Wisdom, drive away from me the darkness of blindness and ignorance; most high and eternal Strength, deliver me; most high and eternal Fortitude, assist me; most high and incomprehensible Light, illuminate me; most high and infinite Mercy, have mercy on me [d].

[c] Syrian Clementine Liturgy.
[d] Gallican, of the time of Charlemagne.

INTERCESSIONS.

1. *For the Church.*

MERCIFULLY receive, O Lord, the prayers of Thy Church; that all adversities and errors may be destroyed, and it may serve Thee in quiet freedom; and give Thy peace in our times, through Jesus Christ our Lord[a].

WE beseech Thee, O Lord, let the strong crying of Thy Church ascend to the ears of Thy loving-kindness; that receiving forgiveness of sins, it may become devout by the working of Thy grace, and tranquil under the protection of Thy power; through Jesus Christ our Lord[b].

LOOK mercifully, O good Shepherd, on Thy flock; and suffer not the sheep which Thou hast redeemed with precious Blood to be torn in pieces by the assaults of the devil[c].

O GOD, Who hast promised that Thou wilt never be absent from Thy Church unto the end of the world, and that the gates of hell shall never prevail

[a] Leonine, as developed in Sarum Daily Office.
[b] Leonine.
[c] Ibid.

against the Apostolic confession; graciously make Thy strength perfect in our weakness, and show the efficacy of Thy Divine promise, while Thou deignest even to be present in Thy feeble ones. For then do we beyond doubt feel Thy presence, when Thou dispensest to each one, at all times, in fitting manner, things desirable, and by perpetual protection guardest us from the attack of all our adversaries [d].

ALMIGHTY and everlasting God, Who hast revealed Thy glory, by Christ, among all nations, preserve the works of Thy mercy; that Thy Church, which is spread throughout the world, may persevere with stedfast faith in the confession of Thy Name; through Jesus Christ our Lord [e].

O GOD, of unchangeable power and eternal light, look favourably on Thy whole Church, that wonderful and sacred mystery; and, by the tranquil operation of Thy perpetual Providence, carry out the work of man's salvation; and let the whole world feel and see that things which were cast down are being raised up, and things which had grown old are being made new, and all things are returning to perfection through Him from Whom

[d] Leonine. [e] Gelasian. The first of the nine solemn Intercessions on Good Friday. Mur. i. 560.

they took their origin, even through our Lord Jesus Christ[f].

O GOD, Who art both the Restorer and the Ruler of mankind; grant, we beseech Thee, that Thy Church may ever be increased by a new offspring, and grow up by the devotion of all the faithful; through Jesus Christ our Lord[g].

O GOD, Who hast made all those that are born again in Christ to be a royal and priestly race[h], grant us both the will and the power to do what Thou commandest; that Thy people who are called to eternal life may have the same faith in their hearts, and the same piety in their actions; through Jesus Christ our Lord[i].

O ALMIGHTY God, we humbly beseech Thee, Who art of boundless goodness, and to be feared for Thy mercy, that by Thine aid all trials, produced by earthly sin or secular danger, may depart from us; and that in Thy Catholic Church religious devotion may ever continue undefiled; through Jesus Christ our Lord[k].

[f] Gelasian. The first of the ten solemn prayers connected with the Lessons of Holy Saturday. Mur. i. 566.

[g] Gelasian.

[h] It is worth observing how the most earnest maintainers of an *external* or hierarchical priesthood have emphatically asserted the *internal* priesthood, or consecrated character of all the baptized. See the second and third Sermons of S. Leo; S. Tho. Aq., Sum. 3. q. 82. a. 1, "Laicus justus unitus est Christo unione spirituali, per fidem et caritatem, non autem per sacramentalem potestatem: et ideo habet spirituale sacerdotium, ad offerendum spirituales hostias;" and Carter on the Priesthood, ch. xiv.

[i] Gelasian.

[k] Gothic.

WE beseech Thee, O Lord, to guide Thy Church with Thy perpetual governance; that it may walk warily in times of quiet, and boldly in times of trouble; through our Lord[l].

MAY Thy Word, O Lord, Which endureth for ever in heaven, abide continually in the Temple of Thy Church; that the presence of the Inhabitant may be an unfailing glory to the habitation; through Thy mercy, &c.[m]

REMEMBER Thy congregation, O Lord, which Thou hast created from the beginning; forget not the Church which of old time Thou hast predestinated in Christ; be mindful of Thy mercy, look upon Thy covenant, and bless us continually with the promised freedom[n].

BEHOLD, O Lord, how Thy faithful Jerusalem rejoices in the triumph of the Cross and the power of the Saviour; grant, therefore, that those who love her may abide in her peace, and those who depart from her may one day come back to her embrace; that when all sorrows are taken away, we may be refreshed with the joys of an eternal resurrection, and be made partakers of her peace world without end; through Thy mercy, &c.[o]

[l] Francic. [m] Mozarabic. [n] Ibid. [o] Ibid.

2. *For Bishops and Pastors.*

O GOD, Who by the power of Thy Majesty dispensest the number of our days and the measure of our time; favourably regard the service which we humbly render; and grant that our times, and those of *N.* our Bishop, may be filled with the abundance of Thy peace and the grace of Thy benignity; through Jesus Christ our Lord[p].

LORD Jesus Christ, Thou didst choose Thine Apostles that they might preside over us as teachers; so also may it please Thee to teach doctrine to *N.* our Bishop[q], in the place of Thine Apostles, and to bless and instruct him, that he may preserve his life unharmed and undefiled for ever and ever[r].

O CHRIST, the true Priest, Whose Priesthood never passeth away, let Thy power come to the aid of Thy servants, and clothe them with glory and beauty, that they may carefully and excellently discharge their priesthood according to

[p] Gelasian. [q] Orig. "*hunc* episcopum."

[r] Pontifical of Egbert. Egbert, brother of King Edbert of Northumbria, became Bishop of York in 734; regained for his see in 735 the Archiepiscopal dignity, which it had lost since the departure of S. Paulinus; and died in 766. He was one of the best and greatest of Saxon prelates, and deservedly loved by Venerable Bede. Some of his writings are given by Johnson in his English Canons. His Pontifical, which has been edited entire by the Surtees Society, contains at p. 33 the versicles, "From our enemies defend us;" and also, at p. 124, a specimen (apparently the earliest) of those indicative Absolutions which Bingham supposed to be not older than the twelfth century,—"Absolvimus vos," &c.

Thy pleasure; and as they have received their talents to be profitably employed, as the Spirit giveth ability, they may at last lay them on Thy table with abundant gain, that they may become worthy to hear that voice full of hope, "Enter into the joy that has no end." May they go on, O Lord, from strength to strength; lift them up while they worship Thee; perfect Thy gifts in them, and crown their heads with a diadem, and in their hearts, as in an ark, may Thy grace be stored up; grant them Thine abundant help, and fill their labours with power [s].

O GOD, Whose ways are all mercy and truth, carry on Thy gracious work, and bestow, by Thy benefits, what human frailty cannot attain; that they who attend upon the heavenly Mysteries may be grounded in perfect faith, and shine forth conspicuous by the purity of their souls; through Jesus Christ our Lord [t].

LORD God of powers, do Thou sanctify the Pastors and Prelates of Thy sheep; that our adversary the devil, overcome by their faith and holiness, may not dare to touch or violate the flock of the Lord; through the same our Lord Jesus Christ [u].

Several of the Prayers for the use of Clergy (see below) may be altered into an intercessory form.

[s] Syro-Nestorian Ordinal. [t] Leonine. [u] Gothic Missal.

3. *For the Sovereign.*

O GOD, in Whose hand are the hearts of kings, incline Thy merciful ears to our humble entreaty; and govern with Thy wisdom our Queen Thy servant[x]; that her counsels may be drawn from Thy fountain, and she may be well-pleasing in Thy sight, and pre-eminent among all Sovereigns; through Jesus Christ our Lord[y].

WE beseech Thee, Almighty God, that Thy servant *Victoria*, who by Thy mercy hath undertaken the government of the realm, may also receive the increase of all virtues, and, being beautified therewith, may be able to avoid the enormity of sin, and to attain to Thee, Who art the Way, the Truth, and the Life, and be acceptable in Thy sight; through Jesus Christ our Lord[z].

4. *For a Family.*

ALMIGHTY and everlasting God, be Thou present to our duties, and grant the protection of Thy presence to all that dwell in this house; that Thou mayest be known to be the Defender of Thy family, and the Inhabitant of this dwelling; through Jesus Christ our Lord[a].

[x] Orig. "Principibus nostris." The prayer ends, "et super omnia regna præcellant." Murat. i. 731.
[y] Gelasian. [z] Gregorian. [a] Gelasian.

HEAR us, holy Lord, Father Almighty, everlasting God, and be pleased to send Thy holy angel from heaven, to guard, cherish, protect, visit, and defend all who dwell in this habitation; through Jesus Christ our Lord [b].

WE beseech Thee, O Lord, make Thy servants alway to join together in seeking Thee with their whole heart, to serve Thee with submissive mind, humbly to implore Thy mercy, and perpetually to rejoice in Thy blessings; through Jesus Christ our Lord [c].

5. *For Relations and Friends.*

STRETCH forth, O Lord, Thy mercy over Thy servants *N. N.*, even the right hand of heavenly help; that they may seek Thee with their whole heart, and obtain what they rightly ask for; through Christ our Lord [d].

O GOD, Who by the grace of the Holy Ghost hast poured the gifts of love into the hearts of Thy faithful people; grant unto Thy servants *N. N.*, for whom I implore Thy mercy, health of body and soul; that they may love Thee with all their

[b] Gelasian.

[c] Ibid. This immediately follows, in a *Missa in Monasterio*, the original form of our Collect for the Clergy and People. That collect was first composed for a monastic community, or for any Christian household, (see Murat. i. 719, 737). The reading then was, "Bestow on Thy servants," &c.

[d] Gelasian.

strength, and with perfect affection fulfil Thy pleasure; through Jesus Christ our Lord [e].

O GOD, Who art pleased to accept the prayers which Thy suppliants offer in discharging the duty of love; grant Thy servants *N. N.* to advance in the love of Thee, and to rejoice in Thy protection; that they may serve Thee with a quiet mind, and be able evermore to abide in Thy peace; through Jesus Christ our Lord [f].

ALMIGHTY and everlasting God, have mercy on Thy servant *N.*, and guide *him* according to Thy clemency into the way of everlasting salvation; that by Thy grace *he* may desire what pleases Thee, and with all power may perform it; through our Lord [g].

O CHRIST, my Creator and Redeemer, Almighty Lord God, forgive all their sins to all who are joined to me by friendship or blood, and for whom I am desired to pray, or have resolved to pray,—and to all Thy faithful people. Deliver them from all evil, preserve them in all good, and bring them to everlasting joy [h].

MOST high God, our loving Father, infinite in majesty, I humbly beseech Thee for Thy ser-

[e] Gregorian. [f] Ibid. [g] Ibid.
[h] From a Prayer in the Corbey MS. in Menard's Notes to the Gregorian Sacramentary.

vant *N.*, that Thou wouldest give *him* a pure mind, perfect love, sincerity in conduct, purity in heart, strength in action, courage in distresses, self-command in character. May *his* prayers ascend to Thy gracious ears, and Thy loving benediction descend upon *him:* that *he* may in all things be protected under the shadow of Thy wings, and my prayers for *him*, through Thy mercy, may not be rejected in Thy gracious presence. Grant *him* pardon of *his* sins; perfect *his* work, accept *his* prayers. Protect *him* by Thine own Name, O God of Jacob! send *him* Thy saving help from Thy holy place, and strengthen *him* out of Sion. Remember *his* offering, accept *his* sacrifice, give *him* the grace of devotion, fulfil *his* desire with good gifts, and crown *him* with mercy. When *he* serves Thee with faithful devotion, pardon *his* sins; and lest *he* should commit things to be repented of, correct *him* with Fatherly tenderness. Grant that being delivered from all adversity, and both here and eternally justified, *he* may praise Thee for ever with the Angels, saying, Holy, Holy, Holy[1].

GRANT Thy servants whom Thou hast united to us by the intimacy of holy affection, or by the ties of blood, or hast associated with us in the unity of faith, to be subject to Thee with their

[1] Gallican Sacramentary.

whole heart; that being filled with the Spirit of Thy love, they may be cleansed from earthly desires, and be made worthy, by Thy grace, of heavenly blessedness [k].

6. *For a Friend before a Journey.*

O GOD, Who bestowest Thy mercy at all times on them that love Thee, and in no place art distant from those that serve Thee; direct the way of Thy servant *N.* in Thy will, that having Thee for *his* Protector and Guide, *he* may walk without stumbling in the paths of righteousness; through Jesus Christ our Lord [l].

HEAR, O Lord, our prayers, and graciously accompany thy servant *N.* on *his* journey; and as Thou art everywhere, do Thou everywhere bestow on *him* Thy mercy, that being by Thine assistance defended against all adversities, *he* may enjoy the fulfilment of *his* just desires; through Jesus Christ our Lord [m].

O GOD of infinite mercy and boundless majesty, Whom no distance of place nor length of time can part from those for whom Thou carest; be present to Thy servants who everywhere confide in Thee; and through all the way in which they are

[k] Gallican, of the tenth century. Martene, i. 557.
[l] Gelasian. [m] Ibid.

to go, be pleased to be their Guide and their Companion. May no adversity harm them, no difficulty oppose them; may all things turn out happily and prosperously for them; that by the aid of Thy right hand, whatsoever they have asked for with a reasonable desire, they may speedily find brought to good effect; through Jesus Christ our Lord[n].

7. *For a Friend in any Danger.*

O GOD, Who justifiest the ungodly, and willest not the death of a sinner; we humbly beseech Thy Majesty that Thou wouldest graciously protect with heavenly aid Thy servant *N.*, who relies on Thy mercy, and keep *him* safe with unceasing protection; that *he* may continually serve Thee, and not be parted from Thee by any temptation; through our Lord Jesus Christ[o].

8. *For a Friend on his Birthday.*

ALMIGHTY and everlasting God, the Maker of all creation, mercifully hear our prayers, and grant many and happy years to Thy servant *N.*, whom Thou didst cause to come forth from *his* mother's womb into this life, that *he* may spend all *his* life so as to please Thee; through Jesus Christ our Lord[p].

[n] Gelasian. [o] Gregorian.

[p] Gelasian. "Oratio in *Natale genuinum.*" There is a regular Mass, with two collects, a *secreta*, *infra actionem*, and Post-communion. The anniversary is mentioned in each. Mur. i. 724.

O GOD, the Life of the faithful, the Saviour and Guardian of those that fear Thee, Who, after the expiration of a year, hast been pleased to bring Thy servant *N.* to this *his* natural birthday; increase in *him* the grace of the Protector of life, and multiply *his* days with many years; that having, by Thy favour, been carried through a happy life, *he* may be enabled to attain the height of heavenly joys; through Jesus Christ our Lord[q].

9. *For the Sick.*

O GOD, Who ever governest Thy creatures with tender affection; incline Thine ear to our supplications, and graciously regard Thy servant, who is suffering from bodily sickness; and visit *him* with Thy salvation, and bestow the medicine of heavenly grace; through Jesus Christ our Lord[r].

O GOD, Who hast vouchsafed to mankind the remedies that bring salvation, and the gifts of eternal life; preserve to Thy servant the gifts of Thy power, and grant that not only in *his* body, but also in *his* soul, *he* may experience Thy healing; through Jesus Christ our Lord[s].

O GOD of heavenly powers, Who by the might of Thy command drivest away from men's bodies all sickness and all infirmity; be present in

[q] Gelasian. [r] Ibid. [s] Ibid.

Thy goodness to this Thy servant, that *his* weakness may be banished and *his* strength recalled, and *his* health being thereupon restored, *he* may bless Thy holy Name, through our Lord Jesus Christ [t].

O GOD, by Whose command the moments of our life run their course; receive our prayers for Thy servants lying sick, on whose behalf we implore Thy mercy; that our fears on account of their danger may be turned into joy at their recovery; through Jesus Christ our Lord [u].

ALMIGHTY and everlasting God, the eternal Salvation of believers, hear us for Thy servants *N. N.*, for whom we implore the aid of Thy mercy; that their health may be restored to them, and they may give thanks to Thee in Thy Church; through Jesus Christ our Lord [x].

O GOD, Who didst add fifteen years to the life of Thy servant Hezekiah; let Thy power raise up Thy servant *N.* from the bed of sickness unto health; through Jesus Christ our Lord [y].

LOOK, O Lord, upon Thy servant *N.*, who is suffering from *his* bodily sickness, and refresh the soul which Thou hast created; that being

[t] Gelasian. [u] Ibid. [x] Ibid. [y] Gregorian.

bettered by Thy chastisement, it may straightway feel itself saved by Thy healing; through Jesus Christ our Lord [a].

O GOD, with Whom it is an easy thing to give life to the dead; restore the sick to their former health, and let none that implore the healing of Thy heavenly mercy be in want of the remedies of earthly medicine; through Jesus Christ our Lord [a].

O CHRIST our Lord, Who art the Physician of salvation, grant unto the sick the aid of heavenly healing. Look upon all faithful people who are sick, and who love to call upon Thy Name, and take their souls into Thy keeping, and vouchsafe to deliver them from all sickness and infirmity [b].

ALMIGHTY and everlasting God, Who succourest those that labour under perils and afflictions, we humbly beseech Thy Majesty, that it may please Thee to send Thy holy Angel to uphold with Thy comfort Thy servant *N.*, who in this house is suffering distress and affliction; that *he* may both receive Thy present aid, and attain eternal healing; through Jesus Christ our Lord [c].

VISIT Thy servant, O Lord, as Thou wast pleased to visit Peter's mother-in-law and the cen-

[a] Gregorian. [a] Gothic. [b] Mozarabic.
[c] Gallican, of the tenth century.

turion's servant. Restore *him*, O Lord, to *his* former health; that *he* may be enabled to say in the courts of Thine house, "The Lord hath chastened and corrected me, but He hath not given me over unto death, He Who is the Saviour of the world." Grant this, O Lord, Who with God the Father and the Holy Spirit livest and reignest, God, throughout all ages [d].

ALMIGHTY and everlasting God, Who succourest those who are suffering in peril and sore need, we beseech Thee that it may please Thee to send Thy holy Angel to raise up Thy servant with consolations, whereby *he* may both receive present aid, and enjoy eternal healing; through Jesus Christ our Lord [e].

SOVEREIGN Lord, our God, Almighty, we beseech Thee to save us all, Thou only Physician of souls and bodies. Sanctify us all, Thou that healest every disease; and heal also this Thy servant. Raise *him* up from the bed of pain by Thy tender mercy; visit *him* in mercy and compassion; drive away from *him* all sickness and infirmity; that being raised up by Thy mighty hand, *he* may serve Thee with all thankfulness; and that we,

[d] Sarum Manual. Part of a Visitation prayer, of which the first words are preserved in our Collect, "Hear us." Until 1661 this Collect retained rather more of the old language, and was, as of old, a prayer to the Son.

[e] York Manual.

being made partakers of Thine ineffable benignity, may praise and glorify Thee, Who doest works great and wonderful, and worthy to be praised. For it is Thine to pity and to save; and to Thee we ascribe glory, Father, Son, and Holy Ghost, now and for ever, and unto ages of ages[f].

MAY the Lord forgive all thy sins and heal all thine infirmities, and save thy life from destruction, and satisfy thy desire in all things, Who only liveth and reigneth, One God in Trinity, through everlasting ages[g].

O LORD, holy Father, Almighty and everlasting God, hear us, and preserve this Thy servant *N.* to whom Thou hast given life, and whom Thou hast redeemed by the price and the great gift of the Blood of Thy Son, Who liveth and reigneth, &c.[h]

WE implore the mercy of Thy Majesty, that it may please Thee to give to this Thy servant *N.* pardon of *his* sins, that *he* being delivered from all the bonds of the enemy may cleave to Thy commandments with *his* whole heart, and evermore love Thee alone with all *his* strength, and one day be counted worthy to attain to the sight of Thy blessedness; through Christ our Lord[i].

[f] Greek Office for the Sick. [g] From Menard's edition of the Gregorian.
[h] From a Rheims MS. cited by Menard. [i] From the same.

10. *For a Sick Person about to Communicate.*

O HOLY Lord, Father Almighty, everlasting God, we entreat Thee in faith that our *brother N.*, receiving the most holy Body and Blood of Thy Son our Lord Jesus Christ, may enjoy health both in body and soul; through the same our Lord[k].

LORD Jesus Christ, our Saviour and Redeemer, hear us when we pray to Thee for our sick *brother N.*, that Thy Holy Eucharist may avail for the preservation of *his* soul and body, and for *his* attainment of eternal life, Who livest, &c.[l]

11. *Litany for the Sick.*

LORD, have mercy upon *him.*
Christ, have mercy upon *him.*
Lord, have mercy upon *him.*
O Christ, hear us[m].
Be merciful, *Spare him, O Lord.*
Be merciful, *Deliver him, O Lord.*
From all evil, *O Lord, deliver him.*
From *his* sins;
From unholy thoughts;
From pain and anguish;
From the snares of the devil;

[k] From a Pontifical of the ninth century. Also in Sarum and York.
[l] From a Pontifical of the twelfth century. Martene, i. 905. And see Menard, p. 343, for a somewhat shorter form from a MS. of the eleventh century.
[m] Here in the original is a series of Invocations.

From the power of demons;
From all tribulation at this time;
From everlasting damnation;
From Thine exceeding dreadful wrath;
By the mystery of Thy holy Incarnation;
By Thine Advent;
By Thy Nativity;
By Thy Baptism;
By Thy Passion and Cross;
By Thy glorious Resurrection;
By Thy wonderful Ascension;
By the grace of the Holy Ghost the Comforter;
In the hour of *his* departure;
We sinners *do beseech Thee to hear us;*

That Thou remove from *him* Thy wrath; *We beseech Thee to hear us, O Lord.*

That it may please Thee to give *him* fruitful and saving penitence;

That it may please Thee to give *him* a humbled and contrite heart;

That it may please Thee to give *him* a fountain of tears;

That it may please Thee to give *him* perfect faith, hope, and love;

That Thou wouldest take away from *him* all murmuring and impatience;

That it may please Thee mercifully to raise *him* up from the bed of sickness;

That it may please Thee to restore *him* in health and safety to Thy holy Church;

That it may please Thee to give *him* pardon of all sins;

That it may please Thee to give *him* Thy grace;

That it may please Thee to give *him* eternal life;

That it may please Thee to bless *him* with Thy holy right hand;

Son of God;

O Lamb of God, That takest away the sins of the world; *Have mercy upon us, and upon him, O Lord*[n].

12. *Prayers for the Dying.*

UNTO Thee, O Lord, we commend the soul of Thy servant *N.*, that dying to the world, *he* may live to Thee; and whatever sins *he* has committed through the frailty of earthly life, do Thou clear away by Thy most loving and merciful forgiveness; through Jesus Christ our Lord[o].

ALMIGHTY and everlasting God, the Guardian of souls, Who in Thy love dost correct, by scourging, those whom Thou receivest; we call upon Thee, O Lord, that it may please Thee to bestow Thy healing on the soul of Thy servant *N.*, who suffers in body from weakness, and the force of

[n] From Gallican and York Litanies for the Sick. See Martene, i. 873, 886; S. Greg. Magn. Op. iii. 546.

[o] Gregorian.

pains, and the pangs of disease. Grant *him*, O Lord, Thy grace, that *his* soul, in the hour of its departure from the body, may attain to be presented by the hands of holy Angels, clear from all stains of deadly sin, unto Thee Who gavest it; through our Lord[p].

ALMIGHTY and everlasting God, Who hast been pleased to breathe into man a soul according to Thy likeness, do Thou, while at Thy bidding dust returns to dust, command Thine image to be associated with Thy Saints and elect in an everlasting home; and gently and tenderly receive it as it returns from the land of Egypt unto Thee, and send Thy holy Angels to meet it, and show it the way of righteousness, and open the gates of Thy glory[q].

SOVEREIGN Lord, our God, Almighty, Who willest that all men should be saved, and come to a knowledge of the truth; Who desirest not the death of a sinner, but rather that he should be converted and live; we pray and beseech Thee, loose

[p] Gallican, of the ninth century. Martene, ii. 1060.

[q] York Manual. In this office and in a Salzburg Pontifical quoted by Martene, ii. 1048, the prayer seems to be prescribed for use at the moment of death. In the Sarum rite it was part of the second Commendation, which was said *after* the passing of the soul. With regard to the clause respecting the land of Egypt, it may be observed that the Psalm "*In exitu Israel*" was often prescribed (as in Sarum and York) to be said at or after the passing, and at the burial; a glorious comment on the triumphant words, "Death is swallowed up in victory." Part of the above prayer is Gelasian, Mur. i. 751, "oratio post sepulturam."

the soul of this Thy servant from every bond, and free it from every curse. For Thou art He that loosest the fettered, and raisest up the crushed, O Thou Hope of the hopeless! Command, therefore, O Lord, that the soul of Thy servant be released in peace, and go to rest in Thine eternal tabernacles with all Thy Saints, through Thine Only-begotten Son; with Whom, and with Thy Holy and life-giving Spirit, Thou art blessed now and ever, and unto ages of ages[r].

13. *Litany for the Dying.*

O GOD the Father, of heaven; *have mercy upon the soul of Thy servant.*

O God the Son, Redeemer of the world;

O God the Holy Ghost;

O Holy Trinity, One God; *Have mercy upon his soul.*

Thou Who art Three and One;

O God the Holy of Holies;

By Thy holy Incarnation;

By Thy holy Nativity;

By Thy holy Circumcision;

By Thy holy Epiphany;

By Thy holy Baptism;

By Thy holy Passion;

[r] Eastern Church Office for the Dying. Euchol., p. 741. "A prayer for a soul going to judgment."

By Thy holy and most loving Death;
By Thy holy Descent into hell;
By Thy glorious Resurrection;
By Thy wonderful Ascension;
By the Coming of the Holy Ghost the Comforter;
By the majesty of Thy Coming;
We sinners *do beseech Thee to hear us.*

That it may please Thee to deliver the soul of Thy servant from the princes of darkness, and the place of punishment; *We beseech Thee to hear us, O Lord.*

That it may please Thee to put all *his* sins out of remembrance for ever;

That it may please Thee mercifully to pardon whatever guilt *he* hath contracted by the fraud of the devil, or by *his* own sinfulness and weakness [a];

That *he* may be enabled by Thy bounty to receive that remission of *his* sins which *he* has ever longed for;

That it may please Thee to give to this our *brother*, returning to Thee out of Egyptian bondage, a place of refreshment, and light, and everlasting blessedness;

That it may please Thee to give *him* joy and

[a] Compare the Gelasian prayer after the Absolution in our Visitation Office, "O most merciful God." It was for ages the established form for the "Reconciliation of dying penitents."

gladness in Thy kingdom, with Thy Saints and elect;

That *he* may with confidence wait for the Day of Judgment;

That it may please Thee to show *him* that sight so full of loveliness[t], Thy holy and glorious Face looking on *him* with benignity;

That it may please Thee to hear us;

Son of God;

O Lamb of God, That takest away the sins of the world; *Have mercy on his soul.*

O Lamb of God, That takest away the sins of the world; *Give him peace, and eternal happiness, and everlasting glory.*

Lord, have mercy upon *him*, &c.[u]

14. *A Final Commendation of the Dying.*

DEPART, O Christian soul, out of this world, in the Name of God the Father Almighty, Who created thee; in the Name of Jesus Christ His Son, Who suffered for thee; in the Name of the Holy Ghost, Who has been poured into thee; may thy place be this day in peace, and thy habitation in the Heavenly Jerusalem[v].

[t] "Desiderabilem." From Cant. v. 16, "Totus desiderabilis," where we read "altogether lovely."
[u] From Litanies of Sarum, Fleury, Jumièges, Rouen.
[v] From the Commendation in Sarum.

15. *For the Afflicted.*

UNTO every Christian soul that is afflicted, or plunged into distress, grant Thou mercy, grant relief, grant refreshment [x].

DESPISE not, O Lord, we beseech Thee, those who cry out in their afflictions, but mercifully relieve their pain with speedy aid; through Jesus Christ our Lord [y].

ALMIGHTY and everlasting God, the Comfort of the sad, the Strength of sufferers, let the prayers of those that cry out of any tribulation come unto Thee; that all may rejoice to find that Thy mercy is present with them in their afflictions; through Christ our Lord [z].

WE beseech Thee, O Lord, give strength to the weary, aid to the sufferers, comfort to the sad, help to those in tribulation [a].

THAT it may please Thee to look upon and to relieve the miseries of the poor and of captives: *We beseech Thee, hear us* [b].

HOW great is Thy mercy, O Lord, in succouring the captives, sparing the wretched, forgiving

[x] Liturgy of S. Mark. [y] Leonine.
[z] Gelasian. Sixth Intercession for Good Friday.
[a] Ambrosian. Mart. iii. 535. From a Processional for the Rogations.
[b] Sarum Litany.

sinners, supporting travellers, relieving the oppressed, hearing prayers, giving to the destitute what they need, converting barbarous nations to the calling upon Thy Name! Be pleased, O loving and merciful God, to hear us when we implore that mercy[c].

O GOD, Who art the Author of love, and the Lover of pure peace and affection, heal the diseases of all Christians who are sick, and let all who are terrified by fears, afflicted by poverty, harassed by tribulation, worn down by illness, given over to punishments, and all prisoners, and wayfarers, be set free by Thine indulgent tenderness, raised up by amendment of life, and cherished by Thy daily compassion[d].

O GOD, our Refuge in pains, our Strength in weakness, our Help in tribulations, our Solace in tears; spare, O Lord, spare Thy people, give not up to beasts the souls that praise Thee[e].

16. *For all in Error or Sin.*

O GOD of heavenly powers, fulfil Thy promised mercy; that the hearts of the rebellious may

[c] Gallican Sacramentary. [d] Ibid.
[e] Ibid. The Vulgate of our Ps. lxxiv. 20. This prayer is in a Mass "in *Letanias* dicenda."

be subdued to the truth of the Gospel; through Jesus Christ our Lord [f].

ALMIGHTY and everlasting God, Who savest all men, and willest not that any should perish; look upon the souls which have been deceived by the fraud of the devil; that all heretical perversity may be driven away, and the hearts of the erring may repent, and return to Thine unshaken truth; through Jesus Christ our Lord [g].

DISSOLVE, O Christ, the schisms of heresy, which seek to subvert the faith, which strive to corrupt the truth; that as Thou art acknowledged in heaven and in earth as one and the same Lord, so Thy people, gathered from all nations, may serve Thee in the unity of faith [h].

GRANT, O Lord, to those who have lost the grace of the Font, that they may again be adorned with the gifts of faithful repentance; through Jesus Christ our Lord [i].

O THOU most clement, Who recallest the erring Thou most merciful, Who despisest not sinners, we rely on Thine own promise, O Lord, that Thou wilt give pardon to the penitent. May all who seek Thee find Thee [k].

[f] Leonine. [g] Gelasian. Seventh Intercession for Good Friday.
[h] Mozarabic. [i] Gallican Missal. [k] Gallican Sacramentary.

HAVE mercy, O Lord, upon Thy servants—that all their wickedness may be put away, and they may be so protected by the defence of Thy compassion, that they may go on to perfection in the keeping of Thy commandments; so that in this life they may avoid all misdeeds, and may one day come without confusion before the presence of Thy glory[l].

THAT Thou wouldest bring back the erring into the way of salvation: *We beseech Thee, hear us*[m].

O GOD, Who delightest in the devotion of the faithful, make Thy people, we pray Thee, to be devoted to Thy holy things; that they who depart from their duties by ungodly depravity of mind, may be converted by Thy grace, and return from the snares of the devil wherein they are held captive; through Jesus Christ our Lord[n].

17. *For Jews and Heathen.*

ALMIGHTY and everlasting God, Who repellest not even the faithless Jews from Thy mercy; hear our prayers, which we offer unto Thee for that blinded people; that by acknowledging the Light of Thy truth, which is Christ, they may be rescued

[l] Gallican Sacramentary. [m] Lyons Litany. [n] Gelasian.

from their own darkness; through the same Jesus Christ our Lord[o].

ALMIGHTY and everlasting God, Who desirest not the death, but always the life of sinners; mercifully receive our prayer, and deliver the Heathen from idolatry, and gather them into Thy holy Church, to the praise and glory of Thy Name; through Jesus Christ our Lord[p].

GRANT, O God, that all the inhabitants of the world may come to be sons of Abraham, and to hold the dignity of Israelites, through Jesus Christ our Lord[q].

I INTREAT Thee, O Lord, holy Father, everlasting God, command the way of Thy truth and of the knowledge of Thee to be shown to Thy servants[r] who wander in doubt and uncertainty amid the darkness of this world; that the eyes of their souls may be opened, and they may acknowledge Thee, the One God, the Father in the Son, and the Son in the Father, with the Holy Spirit, and enjoy the fruit of this confession, both here and in the world to come; through Jesus Christ our Lord[s].

[o] Gelasian. This and the next prayer are the eighth and ninth Intercessions for Good Friday.
[p] Gelasian. [q] Ibid.
[r] Orig., "huic famulo Tuo,"—one who is to become a catechumen.
[s] Gregorian according to Pamelius.

O GOD, Who art rich in mercy to all, O Father of glory, Who madest Thy Son to be a Light to the Gentiles, to proclaim redemption to the captives and sight to the blind; do Thou, Who by Christ art bounteous in compassion, grant them remission of sins, and a portion among the Saints through faith [t].

ALMIGHTY Lord our God, direct our steps into the way of peace, and strengthen our hearts to obey Thy commands: may the Day-spring visit us from on high, and give light to those who sit in darkness and the shadow of death; that they may adore Thee for Thy mercy, follow Thee for Thy truth, desire Thee for Thy sweetness, Who art the blessed Lord God of Israel [u].

18. *A General Pleading.*

WE sinners *do beseech Thee, hear us.*

That it may please Thee to defend and exalt Thy Church; *We beseech Thee, Lord Jesus, to hear us.*

That it may please Thee to grant to Thy Church the tranquillity of peace;

That it may please Thee to put down the enemies of God's Holy Church;

[t] Gallican Sacramentary. [u] A *Collectio post Prophetiam*, i.e. after the *Benedictus*. See Christian Remembrancer, xxv. 475.

That it may please Thee to defend us from dangerous enemies;

That it may please Thee to preserve *N.*, our pastor and chief priest, and the flock committed to him;

That it may please Thee to preserve the Queen in perpetual prosperity;

That it may please Thee to preserve all orders of the Church, the clergy and laity, and the whole people;

That it may please Thee to make us persevere in good works;

That it may please Thee to give us celestial armour against the devil;

That Thy mercy and pity may keep us safe;

That Thou wouldest give us the will and the power[1] to repent in earnest;

That it may please Thee to give us pardon of all sins;

That it may please Thee to give us right faith, firm hope in Thy goodness, and perfect love, and constant fear of Thee;

That it may please Thee to remove evil thoughts from us;

That it may please Thee to pour into our souls the grace of the Holy Spirit;

[1] "Affectum et effectum." Mart. ii. 1066.

That it may please Thee to give us perpetual light;

That it may please Thee to give us a happy end;

That it may please Thee to bring us to everlasting joys;

That it may please Thee to hear us;

Son of God;

O Lamb of God, That takest away the sins of the world; *Spare us.*

O Lamb of God, &c., *Give us pardon.*

O Lamb of God, &c., *Hear us*[y].

GIVE perfection to beginners, give intelligence to the little ones, give aid to those who are running their course. Give compunction to the negligent, give fervour of spirit to the lukewarm, give to the perfect a good consummation[z].

[y] From various Gallican Litanies. See S. Greg. Op. 396; Mart. i. 863; ii. 1066; iii. 457, 525.

[z] Gallican Sacramentary.

PRAYERS
BEFORE CHURCH SERVICE.

O LIFE-GIVING Master, and Bestower of good things, Who hast given unto men the blessed Hope of everlasting life, our Lord Jesus Christ; grant us to perform this Divine service unto Thee in holiness, that we may enjoy the blessedness to come; and being evermore guarded by Thy power, and guided into the light of truth, may continually render unto Thee all glory and thanksgiving [a].

HOLY, Most High, Awful, Who dwellest in the holy place, make us holy, and bring us near to Thee, and cleanse us from all defilement, that we may perform the worship of our fathers in Thy fear; for Thou art He that blesses and hallows all things [b].

LORD God, of might inconceivable, of glory incomprehensible, of mercy immeasurable, of benignity ineffable; do Thou, O Master, look down upon us in Thy tender love, and show forth, towards us and those who pray with us, Thy rich mercies and compassions [c].

[a] Liturgy of S. James. [b] Liturgy of S. Mark.
[c] Liturgy of S. Chrysostom.

O BENIGNANT King of ages and Master of all creation, receive Thy Church approaching Thee through Christ; fulfil for each of us what is good for him; bring us all to perfection, and make us meet for the grace of Thy sanctification, uniting us together in Thy Holy Church, which Thou hast purchased with the precious Blood of Thine Only-begotten Son, our Lord and Saviour Jesus Christ; with Whom, and with Thine All-holy, good, and life-giving Spirit, Thou art blessed and glorified for ever [d].

[d] Liturgy of S. James.

PRAYERS
AFTER CHURCH SERVICE.

O GOD, Who hast sounded in our ears Thy divine and saving oracles, enlighten the souls of us sinners to the full understanding of what has been spoken, that we may not only appear to be hearers of spiritual words, but also doers of good works, following after faith unfeigned, blameless life, and irreproachable conduct; through Jesus Christ our Lord [e].

LORD and Master, Jesus Christ, Co-eternal Word of the Father, made like us in all but sin, for the salvation of our race: enable us to be not only hearers of Thine oracles, but also doers of the word, and to bring forth good fruit, thirty-fold and an hundred-fold, that we may attain the kingdom of heaven: and speedily may Thy compassion overtake us; for in Thee are our glad tidings, O Saviour and Guardian of our souls and bodies, and to Thee we ascribe all glory [f].

O LORD God, Who hast taught us to pray all together, and hast promised to hear the united

[e] Liturgy of S. James. This prayer and the one that follows it are not *final* prayers in the originals. [f] Liturgy of S. Mark.

voices of two or three invoking Thy Name; hear now, O Lord, the prayers of Thy servants unto their salvation, and give us in this world knowledge of Thy truth, and in the world to come life everlasting [g].

REGARD, O Lord, the prayers of Thy family, and grant Thine aid to their humble supplications; that, by means of the assistance which they require, they may persevere in the confession of Thy Name: through Jesus Christ our Lord [h].

WE beseech Thee, O Lord, let the earnest desire of Thine obedient people move Thy pity, and let their faithful supplication obtain Thy mercy; that what they cannot claim by merits they may receive by the abundance of Thy pardon; through Jesus Christ our Lord [i].

O GOD of heavenly powers, Who givest more than we ask or deserve; grant, we beseech Thee, that what we cannot have by reliance on our own deserts may be granted to us by Thy mercy; through Jesus Christ our Lord [k].

MAY Thy perpetual gifts, O Lord, be confirmed to Thy faithful servants, that in receiving

[g] Armenian Liturgy. Compare the Prayer of S. Chrysostom.
[h] Leonine. [i] Ibid.
[k] Ibid. This seems to be the original form of that Gelasian Collect which we use on the Twelfth Sunday after Trinity. Here *mereri* has clearly the sense of 'deserving.'

them they may seek Thee, and in seeking Thee may endlessly receive them; through Jesus Christ our Lord[l].

BLESS, O Lord, Thy family in heavenly places[m], and fill them with Thy spiritual gifts; grant them love, joy, peace, patience, goodness, gentleness, hope, faith, chastity; that being replenished with all Thy gifts, they may attain their desire of coming safe unto Thee; through our Lord[n].

WE beseech Thee, Lord, open Thy heavens, open our eyes: from thence may Thy gifts descend to us; from hence may our hearts look back to Thee. May Thy throne be laid open to us, while we receive the benefits which we implore; may our mind be laid open to Thee, while we render the service which is enjoined to us. Look down from heaven, O Lord, behold and visit this vine which Thy right hand hath planted. Strengthen the weak, relieve the contrite, confirm the strong. Build them up in love, cleanse them with purity, enlighten them with wisdom, keep them with mercy. Lord Jesus, Good Shepherd, Who didst lay down Thy life for the sheep, defend the purchase of Thy Blood. Feed the hungry, give drink to the thirsty, seek for the lost, convert the wan-

[l] Gelasian. [m] Eph. i. 3. [n] Gelasian.

dering, bind up that which is broken. Put forth Thine own hand from heaven, and touch the head of each one (here). May they feel the touch of Thy hand, and receive the joy of the Holy Spirit, that they may remain blessed for evermore[o].

[o] From the Benedictionale of S. Ethelwold. In the "Archæologia," vol. xxiv. He was Bishop of Winchester, A.D. 963—984.

EUCHARISTIC PRAYERS.

1. *Before the Celebration.*

TAKE away from us, we beseech Thee, O Lord, all our iniquities, and the spirit of pride and arrogance, which Thou resistest, and fill us with the spirit of fear, and give us a contrite and humbled heart, which Thou dost not despise,—that we may be enabled with pure minds to enter into the Holy of Holies; through Jesus Christ our Lord [a].

O GOD the Father, Who in Thy great and ineffable love to man didst send Thy Son into the world, to bring back the wandering sheep, turn not away Thy face from us when we approach this Thy tremendous and unbloody Sacrifice; for we trust not to our righteousness, but to Thy gracious compassion, whereby Thou dost redeem our race [b].

O LORD God our Master, reject me not, though defiled by a multitude of sins, for, behold, I approach to this Thy divine and heavenly Mystery. Not as being worthy, but looking only to Thy goodness, I lift up my voice unto Thee. O God, be merciful to me a sinner. I have sinned against

[a] Mozarabic, developed from Leonine. [b] Liturgy of S. James.

heaven and before Thee, and I am not worthy to look upon this Thy holy and spiritual Table, whereon Thine only-begotten Son our Lord Jesus Christ is [c] mystically set forth as a Sacrifice for me a sinner, for one stained with every defilement [d].

O LORD our God, the Bread of Heaven, the Life of the world, I have sinned against Heaven and before Thee, and am not worthy to partake of Thine immaculate Mysteries;—but in Thy Divine tenderness do Thou vouchsafe me by Thy grace to partake of Thy holy Body and precious Blood, without condemnation, unto remission of sins and eternal life [e].

O LORD our God, Who hast called us Christians after the Name of Thine Only-begotten Son, and hast given us Baptism in the Font for the remission of sins; make us, we beseech Thee, worthy now to receive this Communion for the remission of our sins,. and to glorify Thee with thanksgiving [f].

O LORD my God, grant me so to receive [g] the Body and Blood of Thy Son our Lord Jesus

[c] This, like much else in Eastern Liturgies, it said anticipatively: for this prayer comes first in the service. Compare the words "take this Holy Sacrament to your comfort," in the English Liturgy.
[d] Liturgy of S. James. [e] Ibid. [f] Armenian Liturgy.
[g] Compare our Collect of Humble Access; "grant us . . . . so to eat the Flesh," &c.

Christ, that by means thereof I may receive forgiveness of all my sins, and be filled with Thy Holy Spirit, O our God, Who livest and reignest world without end[h].

CLEANSE us, O Lord, from our secret faults, and mercifully absolve us from our presumptuous sins, that we may receive Thy holy things with a pure mind; through Jesus Christ our Lord[i].

GRANT, O Lord, that our bodies may be sanctified by Thy holy Body, and our souls purified by Thine atoning Blood, and that they may avail for the pardon of our offences and remission of our sins. Glory be to Thee for ever, O Lord God[k].

LORD, I am not worthy that Thou shouldest come under my roof, but relying on Thy loving-kindness I draw near to Thine Altar;—a sick man, to the Physician of life; a blind man, to the Light of eternal brightness; poor, to the Lord of heaven and earth; naked, to the King of glory; a sheep, to its Shepherd; a creature, to its Creator; desolate, to the loving Comforter; miserable, to the Merciful; a criminal, to the Giver of pardon; ungodly, to the Justifier; hardened, to the Infuser of grace; beseeching Thine exuberant and infinite mercy, that it may please Thee to heal my

[h] Mozarabic. [i] Leonine.
[k] Syrian Liturgy of S. James. This prayer also resembles our Collect.

weakness, to wash my foulness, to enlighten my blindness, to enrich my poverty, to clothe my nakedness, to bring me back from my wanderings, to console my desolation, to reconcile my guiltiness, to give pardon to the sinner, forgiveness to the miserable, life to the criminal, justification to the dead; so that I may be enabled to receive Thee, the Bread of Angels, the King of kings, and Lord of lords, with such chastity of body and purity of mind, such contrition of heart and plenteous sorrow, such spiritual gladness and heavenly joy, such fear and trembling, such reverence and honour, such faith and humility, such purpose and love, such devotion and thanksgiving, as are due and meet; so that it may profit me unto life eternal and remission of all my sins[1].

O GOD the Father, of heaven, *have mercy upon us.*
O God the Son, Redeemer of the world;
O God the Holy Spirit;
Holy Trinity, One God;
Help us, O God our Saviour;
From the dominion of all vices; *O Lord deliver us.*
From blindness of heart;
From all evil;

[1] Sarum. See Miss. Sar., A.D. 1534, fol. 86. This prayer is mostly taken from one of S. Tho. Aquinas, other parts of which appear in another "Oratio," fol. 87.

We sinners, *do beseech Thee to hear us.*

That Thou spare us; *we beseech Thee to hear us.*

That Thou give us a sure hope;

That Thou vouchsafe us a right faith;

That Thou bestow on us perfect love;

That Thou mortify in us the loathsome forms of all vices;

That Thou quicken us with the excellency of all virtues;

That by Thine Incarnation Thou wouldest open for us an entrance into the Holy of Holies;

That by this most holy Mystery Thou wouldest renew our souls and bodies;

That by it Thou wouldest purify our consciences;

That Thou suffer not this tremendous Mystery to be our condemnation;

That we may handle with pure hands this ineffable Sacrament;

That we may receive it with pure minds;

That by it we may obtain pardon of all sins;

That by it we may be able evermore to cleave unto Thee;

That by it we may be thought worthy to have Thee dwelling in us, and ourselves to dwell in Thee;

That it may please Thee to pour into our hearts the grace of the Holy Spirit;

That it may please Thee to preserve the Christian people who have been redeemed by Thy most precious Blood;

That Thou vouchsafe us a place of repentance [m].

2. *At the Offertory.*

WE give thanks to Thee, O Lord God, Father Almighty, together with Thy Son our Lord God and Saviour Jesus Christ, and the Holy Spirit; and we offer unto Thee this reasonable and unbloody service, which all nations offer unto Thee, O Lord, from the rising of the sun unto the going down thereof, from the north and from the south;—for great is Thy Name in all nations, and in every place incense and sacrifice and oblation are offered unto Thy holy Name [n].

RECEIVE, O Lord, we beseech Thee, the sacrifices of our worship; and by the glorious oblation purify the hearts of those that are subject unto Thee [o].

SEND forth, O Lord, we beseech Thee, the Holy Spirit, to make these present offerings Thy Sacrament unto us, and purify our hearts for its reception [p].

[m] From a Litany in Martene, i. 568, originally edited by Card. Bona, from Card. Chigi's MS. of the tenth century.
[n] Liturgy of S. Mark. See Malachi i. 11. Cf. S. Iren. iv. 17, and Just. Mart. Dial. s. 41. See Lyra Innoc., p. 309, 1st ed.
[o] Leonine. [p] Ibid.

WE beseech Thee, O Lord, in Thy mercy to sanctify these gifts, and having received the offering of the spiritual sacrifice, to make us a perpetual oblation unto Thee; through Jesus Christ our Lord [q].

LOOK mercifully, O Lord, on these present offerings, that they may avail both for our devotion and our salvation; through Jesus Christ our Lord [r].

3. *For the other Communicants.*

REMEMBER, O Lord, Thy servants and handmaids here present [s], whose faith and devotion are discerned and known by Thee [t].

4. *For a Friend.*

HAVE mercy, O Lord, upon Thy servant *N.* for whom I offer this sacrifice of praise to Thy Majesty; that *he* may be able to lead a good life in this world, and happily to attain eternal blessedness [u].

MAY the oblation, O Lord, be of good effect, which I humbly offer to Thy Majesty for the welfare of Thy servant *N.*; that *his* life, amid prosperity and adversity, may everywhere be guided

[q] Leonine. [r] Ibid. [s] "Circumstantium."

[t] Roman Canon; in Gelasian, but doubtless much older. See Palmer, Orig. Lit. i. pp. 117—122. Maskel says, Anc. Lit., p. 88, that this Canon is "undoubtedly older than the third century." He appears to mean, in *substance*; p. xliii.

[u] From two prayers in Gregorian.

by Thy providence; through Jesus Christ our Lord[x].

5. *Before the Consecration.*

CHRIST our Lord and God, being of His own free will made like unto mortals throughout the whole day of this life, showed unto Thee a Body undefiled; and being the fitting Expiator of the ancient offence, exhibited a Soul pure and untouched by sins; and also commanded that as often as His Body and Blood should be received, a Commemoration should be made of the Lord's Passion, which we now make, and proclaim the eternal glory of Jesus Christ Thy Son, our Lord and God; and pray Thee to bless this Sacrifice with Thy blessing, and to sprinkle it with the dew of the Holy Spirit, that it may be to all who receive it a pure, true, and legitimate[y] Eucharist; through Jesus Christ Thy Son, our Lord and God[z].

BE present, be present, Jesus, Good High Priest, in the midst of us, as Thou wast in the midst of Thy disciples. Sanctify this oblation[a].

[x] Gregorian.

[y] *Legitima Eucharistia* is a Gallican phrase, as in "Gothic" services for Circumcision, and Easter Eve, &c. See Neale and Forbes's Gallican Liturgies, p. 4: Mr. Neale takes it rather as "effectual" than as "duly consecrated." See too Lesley on Miss. Moz. 195.

[z] From an ancient Missal edited by Mone. This is perhaps the oldest Liturgy now extant: for it belongs to a time of furious Heathen persecution in the south of Gaul; Mone would say to about A.D. 177. At any rate, it is prior to A.D. 305. See p. 42.

[a] Mozarabic.

6. *After the Consecration.*

THIS is verily and indeed the Body and Blood of Emmanuel our God [b].

HOLY Things for holy persons. There is One holy, One Lord Jesus Christ, to the glory of God the Father, to Whom be glory for ever and ever. Thou Who camest into the world to save sinners, of whom I am the chief—I confess to Thee like the robber, Remember me, Lord, in Thy kingdom [c].

O TRUE Father, behold Thy Son, the Sacrifice well-pleasing to Thee. Through Him Who died for me, be propitious to me. Look on the Blood which was shed on Golgotha by the wicked, and which pleadeth for me; accept my entreaty for its sake. My offences are not greater than Thy compassions; Thy clemency outweighs the hills which Thou weighest in a balance. Behold my sins, but behold also the Sacrifice presented for them; for that Sacrifice is much greater than my guilt. On account of the sins which I have committed, Thy Beloved One endured the nails and spear; His sufferings are enough to propitiate Thee, and to be the means of life to me. Glory be to the Father Who gave up His Son for our salva-

[b] Coptic Liturgy of S. Basil. [c] Liturgy of S. Chrysostom.

tion; and to the Son Who died upon the Cross, and bestowed life upon us all; and to the Spirit Who began and finished the mystery of our salvation. O most high Trinity, spare us all[e]!

WE are guilty, O Father Almighty, through our frequent sins, guilty through the neglect of Thy graces. But from these trespasses of our guilty conscience the Sacrifice of Thine Only Son, offered up to Thee with His Blood, hath cleansed us. And may it also be our succour when we offend after being redeemed, since even until the final day of doom it bestows the grace of repentance on those who do not sin against the Spirit. So may He Who for our redemption made Himself an Advocate with the Father, be Himself the Pleader for our iniquities, even Christ our Lord and eternal Redeemer. Be reconciled, we pray Thee, unto sinners by the Blood of the Righteous One; acknowledge the Victim by Whose intervention Thou hast been propitiated: and receive as Thine adopted children those whose Father Thou hast become through grace[f].

[e] From a Prayer in the Common Order of the Syriac Liturgy.

[f] From two prayers in Mozarabic. This and the preceding Syrian prayer bear witness to the great truth that the Eucharistic Sacrifice, even in its highest aspect, must be put in one line (if we may so say), not with what Christ did once for all upon the Cross, but with what He is doing continually in heaven; that as present naturally in heaven, and sacramentally in the Holy Eucharist, the Lamb of God exhibits Himself to the Father, and *pleads* the Atonement as once finished in act, but ever living in operation; that in neither case does He repeat it or add to it.

O TASTE and see how good the Lord is, Alleluia. Bless the Lord in the heavens, Alleluia. Bless Him in the highest, Alleluia. Bless Him, all ye angels of His, Alleluia. Bless Him, all His host, Alleluia. What blessing or thanksgiving can we offer for this Sacrament? Thee only, O Jesus, do we bless, with the Father and the most Holy Spirit, now and for ever [g].

CHRIST is administering the Bread of the Saints and the Cup of life for remission of sins. Thou art Christ our Lord and Saviour, Who wast born of the Virgin Mary. While we receive this most holy Cup, deliver us for ever from all sin [h].

WE Thy servants, O Lord, bow down our necks before Thy holy Altar, awaiting Thy rich mercies. Send forth upon us, O Lord, Thine abundant grace and benediction, and hallow our souls and bodies and spirits, that we may be made worthy communicants of Thy holy Mysteries, unto remission of sins and eternal life [i].

The notion that it was *not* unique or perfect, but could be reiterated or supplemented, in heaven or on earth, was justly denounced as a "blasphemous fable," in Article XXXI. But this should not lead us to forget that "the Lamb as It had been slain," "appearing in the presence of God for us," "*is* the propitiation for our sins," and even now *tollit peccata mundi*, by an Intercession consisting in the presentation of Himself. See Rev. v. 6, Heb. ix. 24, 1 John ii. 2, and compare Lev. xvi. 11—15. See also the Oxford "Paraphrase" on S. Paul, ed. Jacobson, pp. 365, 373; and the Bishop of Exeter's Pastoral of 1851, pp. 53, 54.

[g] Armenian. [h] Ambrosian. [i] Liturgy of S. James.

UNTO Thee we commend our whole life and hope, O Lord, the Lover of men, and beseech, and pray, and entreat Thee to grant that we may partake of Thy heavenly and awful Mysteries from this holy and spiritual Table with a pure conscience, unto remission of sins, and pardon of transgressions, and communion of the Holy Spirit, and inheritance of the kingdom of heaven, and confidence towards Thee, and not to judgment nor condemnation[k].

GRANT, O Lord Jesus Christ, that the Sacrament of Thy Body and Blood, which I, though unworthy, receive, may not be to me a means of judgment and condemnation, but helpful through Thy loving-kindness to the salvation of my body and soul[l].

MAY Thy spotless Body be the means of my life, and Thy holy Blood of cleansing and remission of my sins[m].

7. *After Communicating.*

O GOD, Who of Thy deep and ineffable love to man hast condescended to the weakness of Thy servants, and made us partakers of this heavenly Table; condemn not us sinners after the reception of Thy spotless Mysteries, but guard us, of

[k] Liturgy of S. Chrysostom. [l] Sarum. [m] Armenian.

Thy goodness, in the sanctification of the Holy Spirit; that being made holy, we may find our portion and inheritance with all the Saints who have pleased Thee from the beginning, in the light of Thy countenance, through the mercies of Thine Only-begotten Son our Lord God and Saviour Jesus Christ [n].

THOU hast given us, O Lord, sanctification by the Communion of the most holy Body and precious Blood of Thine Only-begotten Son; grant us the grace and gift of Thy Holy Spirit, and keep us unreproved in life, and lead us on to the perfect adoption and redemption, and the eternal joys to come [o].

WE thank Thee, loving Master, Benefactor of our souls, for having this day admitted us to Thy heavenly and immortal Mysteries. Guide our path aright; establish us in Thy fear; watch over our life; make safe our goings [p].

WE give Thee thanks, O Lord our God, after having received Thy holy, spotless, immortal, and heavenly Mysteries, which Thou hast given us for the benefit, sanctification, and healing of our souls and bodies. And we pray and beseech Thee, O good Lord, the Lover of men, to grant that the

[n] Liturgy of S. James. [o] Ibid. [p] Liturgy of S. Chrysostom.

Communion of the holy Body and precious Blood of Thine Only-begotten Son may procure for us faith that needeth not to be ashamed, love without dissimulation, fulness of wisdom, healing of soul and body, repulse of every enemy, fulfilment of Thy commandments, an acceptable defence before the awful judgment-seat of Thy Christ[q].

WHAT blessing, or what praise, or what thanksgiving, can we render to Thee, O God, the Lover of men, for that when we were cast away by the doom of death, and drowned in the depth of sin, Thou hast granted us freedom, and bestowed on us this immortal and heavenly food, and manifested to us this Mystery hid from ages and from generations? Grant us to understand this Thy supreme act of mercy, and the greatness of Thy benignity and Fatherly care for us[r].

LEAD us not into temptation, since we have been partakers of the holy Body and precious Blood. And we thank Thee that Thou hast made us meet communicants of the Mystery of glory and holiness which passeth all understanding[s].

LORD Jesus Christ, Who hast given unto us such Food of Thy goodness unto salvation and

[q] Liturgy of S. Basil. This prayer is developed in S. Mark's Liturgy. Compare Neale's Liturgies, pp. 31, 172.
[r] Coptic Liturgy of S. Cyril. [s] Ethiopic.

life eternal, preserve us by means of this Food in purity and without defilement, dwelling within us by Thy divine protection. Guide us by Thy divine grace into the path of Thy holy will, which desires our good, and by it may we be fortified against all the assaults of our enemies, that we may be accounted worthy to hear Thy voice, and to follow Thee, the only mighty and true Shepherd, and to obtain the place prepared in Thy heavenly kingdom, O our God and Saviour Jesus Christ [t].

LIGHT of Light, and God of God, Who didst bow Thy holy heavens, and descend to earth for the salvation of the world, out of Thy love of man; extend Thine Almighty right hand, and send out Thy blessings on us all. Hallow our bodies and souls by this Sacrifice which we have received, and guide our steps into the paths of righteousness, that we may behave ourselves according to Thy will, and observe Thy commandments and do them all the days of our life, and come to a blessed end, and sing a ceaseless hymn with Thy Saints to Thee, and Thy Father, and Thy Holy Spirit [u].

GRANT, O Lord, that what we have taken with our mouth we may receive with our soul, and let that which has been a temporary gift become to

[t] Armenian.

[u] Liturgy of Dioscorus.

us an everlasting remedy; through Jesus Christ our Lord [x].

POUR down upon us, O Lord, the Spirit of Thy love, that Thou mayest preserve in the same piety those whom Thou hast satisfied with the same heavenly Bread [y].

HAVING received life by the refreshment of the most holy Body and Blood of our Lord Jesus Christ, we humbly beseech Thee, O God, that by this transcendent remedy Thou wouldest both cleanse us from the contagion of all sins, and fortify us against the incursion of all dangers; through the same Jesus Christ our Lord [z].

WE render thanks and praise to Thee, O Lord, Who hast strengthened us with the Communion of the Body and Blood of Thy most dearly beloved Son; humbly beseeching Thy mercy that this Thy Sacrament, O Lord, may not increase our guilt and punishment, but may plead for our pardon and salvation. May it be the abolition of our sins, the strength of our weakness, our bulwark against the perils of the world. May this Communion cleanse us from guilt, and make us partakers of the joy of heaven: through Jesus Christ our Lord [a].

[x] Leonine. [y] Ibid. At Easter, "with the Paschal Sacraments." Greg. Sacr. [z] Leonine. [a] Ibid.

MAY the sacred Feast of Thy Table, O Lord, alway strengthen and renew us, guide and protect our weakness amid the storms of the world, and bring us into the haven of everlasting salvation; through Jesus Christ our Lord [b].

VISIT, we beseech Thee, O Lord, Thy family, and guard with watchful tenderness the hearts which have been hallowed by sacred Mysteries; that as by Thy mercy they receive the healing Gifts of eternal salvation, they may retain them by Thy protecting power; through Jesus Christ our Lord [c].

DEFEND, O Lord, with Thy protection those whom Thou satisfiest with heavenly Gifts; that being set free from all things hurtful, we may press onwards with our whole heart to the salvation which cometh from Thee; through Jesus Christ our Lord [d].

WE have received, O Lord, the glorious Mysteries, and pray Thee by means of them to make us partakers of things heavenly, while we are dwelling on the earth; through Jesus Christ our Lord [e].

WE beseech Thee, O Lord, that the solemn reception of Thy Sacrament may cleanse

[b] Leonine. [c] Ibid. [d] Ibid. [e] Ibid.

us from all our old sins, and change us into new creatures; through Jesus Christ our Lord[f].

BEING filled with the very essence of restoration and life, we beseech Thee, O Lord our God, that by the heavenly Gifts which Thou art pleased to bestow on us, Thou wouldest grant us to cleave to things heavenly; through Jesus Christ our Lord[g].

REFRESHED with the participation of the sacred Gift, we beseech Thee, O Lord our God, that we may feel the effectual working of the rite which we celebrate; through the same Jesus Christ our Lord[h].

HEAR, O Lord, our prayers, that the Holy Communion of our redemption may both bestow on us aid for this life, and procure for us everlasting joys; through Jesus Christ our Lord[i].

BEING strengthened with the Gift of our redemption, we beseech Thee, O Lord, that true faith may ever make it a help towards our everlasting salvation; through Jesus Christ our Lord[k].

MAY the holy Food and Drink be salutary to us, O Lord; may it fortify our temporal life,

[f] Leonine. [g] Ibid. [h] Ibid. [i] Ibid. [k] Ibid.

and give us life eternal; through Jesus Christ our Lord[l].

O GOD, Who touchest us in the participation of Thy Sacrament, work out in our hearts the effects of its power, that through Thy Gift itself we may be fitted for the reception of the same; through Jesus Christ our Lord[m].

MAY the heavenly Mystery, O Lord, be to us a renewal of soul and body; and as we have gone through the performance of it, may we feel its effect, through Jesus Christ our Lord[n].

WE thank Thee, O Lord, Who refreshest us both with the partaking of the heavenly Sacrament and with the solemn remembrance of Thy righteous servants, through Jesus Christ our Lord[o].

MAY Thy Table, O God, set us free from earthly delights, and ever supply us with celestial food; through Jesus Christ our Lord[p].

MAY the vices of our hearts be overcome by this Medicine, which came to heal the diseases of our mortal nature[q].

ALMIGHTY and everlasting God, preserve the works of Thy mercy, and pour into our hearts

[l] Leonine. [m] Ibid. [n] Ibid. [o] Ibid, for a Saint's day. [p] Gelasian. [q] Ibid.

the sweetness of the Body and Blood of Thine Only-begotten Son Jesus Christ our Lord [r].

MAY the Communion of Thy Sacrament, O Lord, both purify us and make us one, through Jesus Christ our Lord [s].

DELIVER us from evil, Lord Jesus Christ! We eat Thy Body, which was crucified for us, and we drink Thy Blood, which was shed for us: may Thy holy Body prove our salvation, and Thy holy Blood the forgiveness of our sins, both now and for ever [t].

BEING fed with heavenly Food, and refreshed with the eternal Cup, let us give unceasing thanks and praise to the Lord our God, entreating that we, who have spiritually received the most holy Body of our Lord Jesus Christ, may be freed from carnal vices and be made spiritual [u].

O GOD, Who art eternal salvation, and inestimable blessedness, grant, we beseech Thee, to all Thy servants, that we who have received things holy and blessed, may be enabled to be holy and blessed evermore [x].

O GOD of righteousness, God of mercy, God of immortality and life, God of brightness and glory, we pray and beseech Thee, that being

[r] Gelasian. [s] Ibid. [t] Gothic. [u] Ibid. [x] Ibid.

refreshed by Divine gifts, we may be preserved by Thee for Thyself unto the bliss which is to come; through Jesus Christ our Lord[y].

LOOK upon us, O Lord, Who willest us both to feed on Thy Body and to become Thy Body[z]; grant that what we have received may avail for remission of our sins: and may the Divine sustenance, constituted by Thy benediction, so unite itself to our souls, that the flesh being subdued to the spirit, may obey, and not rebel[a].

O GOD, the Bread of our life, look upon us; be Thou the Guardian of our bodies; be Thou the Saviour of our souls[b].

BELIEVING that we have received from the holy Altar the Body and Blood of Christ our Lord and God, let us pray to the Unity of the Blessed Trinity, that it may be granted to us evermore, in fulness of faith, to hunger and thirst after righteousness; and that we, being strengthened with the grace of the saving Food, may so do His work, that we may possess the Sacrament which we have received, not for judgment, but for healing, through our Lord Jesus Christ[c].

[y] Gothic. [z] Meaning, that the life of the Church, as Christ's Body mystical, is kept up by the Sacramental Communion of His Body and Blood. [a] Gallican Missal. [b] Ibid. [c] Ibid.

O LORD my God, Father, Son, and Holy Spirit, make me ever to seek and love Thee, and by this Holy Communion which I have received never to depart from Thee; for Thou art God, and beside Thee there is none else, for ever and ever[d].

TASTING, O Lord, the fullness of Thy perfect sweetness, we beseech Thee that it may be to us for remission of sins and health of soul, through Thy mercy, &c.[e]

RECEIVING the Cup of the Lord's Passion, and tasting the sweetness of His most holy Body, let us give thanks and praise to Him, walking in His house with joy and gladness[f].

WE have received the Body of Christ, and drunk His Blood. We will fear no evil, for the Lord is with us. May Thy Blood be alway life to us, and salvation of our souls, O our God[g].

LORD our God, mercifully grant that we who have received the Body and Blood of Thine Only-begotten Son, may be far removed from the blindness of the unfaithful disciple, seeing that we confess and worship Christ our Lord, Very God and Man[h].

PRESERVE in us, O Lord, the gift of Thy grace; that by the power and virtue of the

[d] Mozarabic. [e] Ibid. [f] Ibid. [g] Ambrosian. [h] Ibid.

Eucharist which we have received, we may be fortified against all evils of this life and of the life to come[i].

I GIVE Thee thanks, O Lord, holy Father, Almighty, everlasting God, Who hast refreshed me with the most holy Body and Blood of Thy Son Jesus Christ our Lord; and I pray that this Sacrament of our salvation, which I, unworthy sinner, have received, may not turn to my judgment nor condemnation, according to my deserts, but to the profit of my body and soul, unto life eternal[k].

LORD Jesus Christ, Almighty and everlasting God, be merciful to my sins through my reception of Thy Body and Blood. For Thou hast said, "He that eateth My Flesh and drinketh My Blood dwelleth in Me, and I in Him." Therefore I humbly beseech Thee to create in me a clean heart, and renew a right spirit within me, and strengthen me with Thy free Spirit, and cleanse me from all vices and the crafts of the devil, that I may attain to the partaking of heavenly joys; Who livest and reignest, &c.[l]

I BESEECH Thee, O Lord, that this Holy Communion may be my guide, and my food for the journey, unto the haven of eternal salvation. May

[i] Missal published by Matthias Flaccus Illyricus in 1557.
[k] Sarum.
[l] Sarum.

it be to me a consolation while I am harassed in thoughts, a source of sweetest love in the time of good purposes, patience in tribulation and distress, medicine in sickness. By these most sacred Mysteries which I have received, grant me right faith, firm hope, and perfect love, strength to renounce the world, purification of desires, inward sweetness, ardent love for Thee, a recollection and tender sympathy for the Passion of Thy beloved Son, and grace to keep my life full of virtue in the praise of Thee and in sincere faith. And grant me in the hour of my departure to receive the gift of so great a Mystery with true faith, certain hope, and sincere love, that I may see Thee without end[m].

8. *For a Friend.*

MAY Thy Sacrament, O Lord, which I have received, be my cleansing; and grant Thy servant *N.* to be delivered from all sin, that *he* may rejoice in the fullness of the heavenly remedy; through Jesus Christ our Lord[n].

BY the virtue of this Mystery, I beseech Thee, O Lord, to guard Thy servant *N.* with perpetual protection; that *he* may serve Thee with an undistracted mind, and be quiet from fear of evil under Thy shelter; through Jesus Christ our Lord[o].

[m] Sarum. [n] Gregorian. [o] From two Prayers in Gregorian.

BAPTISMAL PRAYERS[a].

O GOD, Who restorest human nature to a higher than its original dignity, look on the ineffable mystery of Thy loving-kindness; and in those whom Thou hast been pleased to renew by the mysteries of regeneration, preserve the gifts of Thy perpetual grace and blessing; through Jesus Christ our Lord[b].

O GOD, Who openest the entrance of the kingdom of heaven to those only who are born again of Water and the Holy Spirit, increase evermore on Thy servants the gifts of Thy grace; that they who have been cleansed from all sins, may not be defrauded of any promises; through our Lord Jesus Christ[c].

O GOD, Who hast renewed in the Font of Baptism those that believe in Thee, vouchsafe to the regenerate in Christ such preserving grace, that they may not lose the grace of Thy benediction by any incursion of error; through the same Jesus Christ our Lord[d].

[a] These Prayers, which strikingly illustrate our Baptismal Offices, clearly assert two things; 1. the reality of Baptismal Regeneration; 2. the necessity of post-baptismal growth in grace.
[b] Gelasian. [c] Ibid. [d] Ibid.

O GOD, Who restorest us unto eternal life by Christ's Resurrection, fulfil the ineffable mystery of Thy loving-kindness; that when our Saviour shall come in His majesty, as Thou hast made us to be regenerated in Baptism, so Thou mayest make us to be clothed with a blessed immortality; through the same our Lord Jesus Christ[e].

O GOD, by Whom redemption cometh to us, and adoption is bestowed, look upon the works of Thy mercy; that unto those who are regenerated in Christ may be vouchsafed both an eternal inheritance and a true freedom; through the same Jesus Christ our Lord[f].

ALMIGHTY and everlasting God, bring us to the fellowship of heavenly joys; that Thou mayest vouchsafe an entrance into Thy kingdom to those that are born again of the Holy Ghost, and that the lowly flock may reach that place whither the mighty Shepherd hath gone before; through the same Jesus Christ our Lord[g].

HEAR us, O Almighty God; and as Thou hast bestowed on Thy family the perfect grace of Baptism, so do Thou dispose their hearts to the attainment of eternal bliss; through Jesus Christ our Lord[h].

[e] Gelasian. [f] Ibid. [g] Ibid. [h] Ibid.

O GOD, Who by the Baptism of Thine Only-begotten Son hast been pleased to sanctify the streams of water; grant that we who are born again of Water and the Spirit may attain an entrance into eternal joys; through the same Jesus Christ our Lord[i].

MAY Thy servants, O Lord, who have been called to Thy grace, be unceasingly protected by Thy help; that they who have been regenerated in divine Baptism, may never be plucked away from the power of Thy kingdom; through Jesus Christ our Lord[k].

O GOD, by Whom redemption and adoption are bestowed upon us, raise up unto Thyself the hearts of Thy believing people; that all who have been regenerated in holy Baptism may apprehend in their minds what they have received in mysteries; through Jesus Christ our Lord[l].

O LORD God Almighty, Who hast commanded Thy servants to be born again of Water and the Holy Ghost, preserve in them the holy Baptism which they have received, and be pleased to perfect it unto the hallowing of Thy Name; that Thy grace may ever increase upon them, and that

[i] Gregorian, as edited by Pamelius. [k] Gothic.
[l] Old Gallican Missal.

what they have already received by Thy gift, they may guard by integrity of life[m].

O GOD, Who hast bestowed on Thy servant by holy Baptism redemption from his sins, and the life of regeneration; do Thou, O Lord God, grant the brightness of Thy face to shine for ever on his heart. Preserve the shield of his faith safe from the lying-in-wait of the adversaries; the robe of incorruption, which he has put on, clean and unpolluted; and the spiritual seal of grace untouched and inviolate; Thou being reconciled to him and us, according to the multitude of Thy mercies;—for blessed and glorified is Thy venerable and majestic Name of Father, Son, and Holy Spirit, now and ever, and unto ages of ages. Amen[n].

O LORD our God, our Master, Who by the font of Baptism dost illuminate the baptized with heavenly radiance, Who hast vouchsafed to Thy servant, (recently illuminated,) by Water and the Spirit, remission of his sins, voluntary and involuntary; lay Thy mighty hand upon him, and protect him with the power of Thy goodness; preserve him from losing the earnest of glory, and be pleased to bring him to eternal life and to Thy

[m] Gallican Sacramentary.
[n] From the Baptismal Rites of the Eastern Church.

good pleasure;—for Thou art our sanctification, and to Thee we render glory, Father, Son, and Holy Ghost, now and ever, and unto ages of ages. Amen[o].

HIM who hath put on Christ our God, do Thou preserve, as an invincible wrestler, against the vain assaults of his adversaries and ours; and grant that all they who are adorned with the incorruptible crown may be victorious even unto the end;—for it is Thine to pity and to save, and to Thee we render glory, with Thine unbegotten Father, and Thy most holy, good, and life-giving Spirit, now and ever, and unto ages of ages. Amen[p].

[*With slight alterations, any of these Prayers will serve for a Baptismal birthday.*]

[o] From the Baptismal Rites of the Eastern Church. [p] Ibid.

PRAYERS FOR SEVERAL OCCASIONS.

1. *For the New Year.*

MAY Christ our Lord, Who is the Head of every beginning, grant us so to pass through the coming year with faithful hearts, that we may be able in all things to please His loving eyes. O God, Who art the Self-same, Whose years shall not fail, grant us to spend this year as Thy devoted servants, according to Thy good pleasure. Fill the earth with fruit, grant our bodies to be free from disease, our souls from offences; take away scandals, and keep far from our borders all manner of calamitous events; through Jesus Christ Thy Son our Lord [a].

2. *Dedication or Opening of a Church.*

O GOD of all sanctification, Almighty Sovereign, Whose goodness is felt to be infinite; O God, Who art present throughout all things at once, in heaven and earth, keeping Thy mercy for Thy people who walk before the presence of Thy glory; hear the prayers of Thy servants, that Thine eyes may be open upon this house day and

[a] Mozarabic.

night; graciously dedicate this church, (set apart by holy rites in honour of Saint *N.*,) mercifully illumine and brighten it with Thine own glory. Favourably accept every one who comes to worship in this place; graciously be pleased to look down, and for the sake of Thy great Name, and strong hand, and high arm, readily protect, hear, and everlastingly keep and defend, those who make their prayer in this habitation; that they being always happy, and always rejoicing in Thy true religion, may constantly persevere in the Catholic Faith of the Holy Trinity; through Jesus Christ our Lord[b].

O GOD, Who although Thou art wholly present everywhere, and containest all things with Thine own Majesty, yet hast willed that places suitable for Thy Mysteries should be consecrated unto Thee, that the houses of prayer should themselves stir up the minds of Thy suppliants to call upon Thy Name; pour out Thy grace upon this place, and show to all who hope in Thee the gift of Thine aid; that here they may obtain both the virtue of Thy Sacraments, and the effect of their own prayers; through Jesus Christ our Lord[c].

O GOD, Who art the Author of all gifts which are to be consecrated unto Thee, be pleased in

[b] Gelasian. [c] Ibid.

Thy goodness to be present for the sanctification of this place; that they who have built it in honour of Thy Name may be enabled to have Thee for their Protector in all things; through Jesus Christ our Lord [d].

WE beseech Thee, O Almighty God, that in this place, which we, though unworthy, dedicate to Thy Name, Thou wouldest incline Thy gracious ears to all who seek Thee; through Jesus Christ our Lord [e].

GRANT, we beseech Thee, O Lord, to our prayers, that all we who enter this temple, (the dedication of which we celebrate on this anniversary,) may please Thee with full and perfect devotion of soul and body; that while we now render to Thee our prayers, we may by Thy help be enabled to attain Thine eternal rewards; through our Lord Jesus Christ [f].

O GOD, Who buildest for Thy Majesty an eternal habitation out of living and elect stones, assist Thy suppliant people, that as Thy Church gains in material extent, it may also be enlarged by spiritual increase; through Jesus Christ our Lord [g].

[d] Gelasian. [e] Gregorian. [f] Ibid. [g] Ibid.

3. *In Time of War.*

ALMIGHTY and merciful God, we beseech Thee to give us rest from the storm of war; for Thou wilt bestow on us all good things if Thou givest us peace both of soul and body; through Jesus Christ our Lord[h].

BEHOLD, O God our Defender, and protect us from fear of the enemy; that all disturbance being removed, we may serve Thee with minds free from distraction; through Jesus Christ our Lord[i].

WE beseech Thee, O Lord, be gracious to our times; that both national quietness and Christian devotion may be duly maintained by Thy bounty; through Jesus Christ our Lord[k].

ALMIGHTY and everlasting God, we pray Thee to crush the force of our enemies; that we may be able to celebrate Thy holy service with undisturbed minds; through Jesus Christ our Lord[l].

WE beseech Thee, O Lord, let the invincible defence of Thy power be the bulwark of Thy faithful people; that they, being ever devoted to Thee with pious affection, may both be freed from the assault of enemies, and continually persevere in Thy grace; through Jesus Christ our Lord[m].

[h] Leonine. Ibid. [k] Ibid. [l] Ibid. [m] Gelasian.

O GOD, the Maker of the universe, by Whose command the course of the world proceeds; be present, in Thy goodness, to our prayers, and vouchsafe in our times the tranquillity of peace; that we may with unceasing exultation rejoice in giving praise to Thy mercy; through Jesus Christ our Lord[n].

4. *In Time of Pestilence or any Affliction.*

LOOK mercifully, O Lord, we beseech Thee, on the affliction of Thy people; and let not our sins prevail to destroy us, but rather Thine abundant mercy to save us, through Jesus Christ our Lord[o].

O GOD, Who desirest not the death, but the repentance of sinners, we beseech Thee, in Thy loving-kindness, to turn Thy people to Thyself; that when they devote themselves to Thee, Thou mayest remove the scourges of Thine anger; through Jesus Christ our Lord[p].

WE beseech Thee, O Lord, mercifully to drive away from Thy faithful, together with their own errors, the destructive fury of disease; that as Thou deservedly scourgest them when they go astray, Thou mayest cherish them with Thy pity when they are brought back; through Jesus Christ our Lord[q].

[n] Gelasian. [o] Leonine. [p] Gelasian. [q] Ibid.

WE beseech Thee, O Lord, give effect to our devout supplication, and mercifully turn away the famine (*or* the pestilence); that the hearts of men may know that these scourges both proceed from Thine indignation, and cease by Thy compassion; through Jesus Christ our Lord[r].

WE beseech Thee, Almighty God, to receive with Fatherly tenderness Thy people fleeing from Thine anger to Thyself; that they who dread the scourge that comes from Thy Majesty may be enabled to rejoice in Thy forgiveness; through Jesus Christ our Lord[s].

HEAR, O Lord, our prayers, and enter not into judgment with Thy servants; for as no righteousness is found in us on which we could rely, so we acknowledge Thee the Fountain of pity[t] whereby we trust both to be cleansed from our sins, and delivered from our distresses; through Jesus Christ our Lord[u].

O GOD, whose loving-kindness is so transcendant, that from the conversion of one sinner Thou causest the utmost rejoicing to take place in heaven; look on this small portion of Thy people, that all affliction may be removed, and Thine inheritance

[r] Gelasian. [s] Ibid.
[t] See the *Dies Iræ;* "Salva me, Fons pietatis." [u] Gelasian.

may increase in numbers and advance in devotion; through Jesus Christ our Lord[x].

WE beseech Thee, O Lord, in Thy compassion, to turn away from Thy people Thy wrath, which indeed we deserve for our sins, but which in our human frailty we cannot endure; therefore embrace us with that tenderness which Thou art wont to bestow on the unworthy; through Jesus Christ our Lord[y].

O GOD, Who scourgest our faults with strokes of love, in order to cleanse us from our iniquities; grant us both to profit by Thy strokes, and speedily to rejoice in Thy consolation[z].

LET our soul bless Thee, O Lord, at all times, because, even when Thou scourgest us, Thy mercy is always present, while Thou both correctest us with discipline and cherishest us with forgiveness; while Thou healest in smiting, and strengthenest in healing; grant therefore unto us, that we who have tasted of Thy sweetness by faith, may enjoy the fullness of Thy delights in the day of retribution; through Thy mercy, &c.[a]

[x] Gelasian. [y] Ibid.
[z] Gregorian. Prescribed for the "Greater Litany" or processional supplication, instituted by S. Gregory on S. Mark's day. Mur. ii. 80; Menard, p. 91. [a] Mozarabic.

SPARE and forgive us, O benignant Master; stay the scourge which is deservedly coming down upon us. Let the multitude of Thy compassions overcome the hateful mass of our sins; let the great deep of Thine infinite goodness cover the bitter sea of our wickedness. We have eminent examples of Thy benignity in robbers, and harlots, and publicans, and the prodigal son; like them we also make our confession unto Thee and fall down before Thee; receive us, O Master, and although we fall far short of their conversion and their sincere repentance, let Thine infinite goodness make up for the defect, yea, make up for everything, for in everything we utterly fall short. Every scourge and plague, and every form of destruction, which is bearing down upon us, is slight and small in comparison of our innumerable transgressions. Wherefore on account of the multitude of our sins we have no ground of confidence, O Lord the righteous Judge, whereon to supplicate of Thy goodness a relief from this terrible menace,—but the exceeding greatness of Thy tenderness and the abyss of Thy compassions, O Master full of pity, compel us boldly to entreat what is beyond our deservings. For this cause, O God of exceeding goodness, O Lord of mercy, we beseech Thee, of Thy gentleness, to stay this sharp sword of untimely death. Accept, O benignant Lord, the common contrition and heart-felt sorrow of us all, as Thou didst accept the tears of Hezekiah in the affliction of his heart, and didst rescue him from death. Remember, O benignant One, Thy Cross and Death and voluntary Passion, which Thou didst endure for us the condemned. From Thee alone do we beg assistance and relief from these horrors; for with Thee alone are possible the things which are impossible with man. Blessed art Thou for ever[b].

O LORD of exceeding goodness, Maker of the universe, Whose mercy is immeasurable, Whose benignity is incomprehensible, Who didst take away all our iniquities and nail them to Thy Cross, that Thou, the sinless One, mightest sanctify us; before Thee we venture to fall down in supplication, O forbearing Lord, and looking upon the great deep of Thine ineffable and immeasurable benignity, to cry unto Thee, our Lord, Who art easy to be reconciled, "Save us." Not in the spirit of the Pharisee, but in the spirit of the Publican, do we offer Thee our worship[c]; nor do we imitate that heartless robber, but like that other good-hearted and grateful one, we cry to Thee with the prayer, "Remember." Remember us, O Lord, in mercy and compassions; send down to us the holy guardian Angel to whom Thou hast

[b] Eastern Church Office, in time of Pestilence.
[c] In the original, "our hymns and canticles."

entrusted our life, that he may rescue us from this terrible raging death, and this unexpected sword; that through this deliverance and release, we may glorify Thee[d].

5. *Thanksgiving on Removal of Calamities.*

ALMIGHTY and everlasting God, Who healest us by chastening, and preservest us by pardoning; grant unto Thy suppliants, that we may both rejoice in the comfort of the tranquillity which we desired, and also use the gift of Thy peace for the effectual amendment of our lives; through Jesus Christ our Lord[e].

WE do not keep silence, O Lord, from praising Thee; because by releasing us from the evils which we deserved, Thou enablest us to celebrate Thy good gifts with gladness; through Jesus Christ our Lord[f].

WE render thanks to Thee, O Lord, Who relievest us from the pressure of temporal affliction, that Thou mayest set us forward on the way to everlasting joys; through Jesus Christ our Lord[g].

WE intreat Thy mercy with our whole heart, that as Thou defendest us against things ad-

[d] From Eastern Church Prayers in Time of Public Calamity.
[e] Leonine. [f] Ibid. [g] Ibid.

verse to the body, so Thou wilt set us free from the enemies of the soul; and as Thou grantest us to rejoice in outward tranquillity, so vouchsafe to us Thine inward peace; through Jesus Christ our Lord[h].

WE beseech Thee, O Lord our God, that the relief from anxiety which Thy mercy has bestowed upon us may not make us negligent, but rather cause us to become more acceptable worshippers of Thy Name; through Jesus Christ our Lord[i].

WE humbly beseech and implore Thy Majesty, O Lord, that as Thou hast delivered us from impending dangers, so Thou wouldest graciously absolve us from our sins; that Thou mayest both bestow upon us greater benefits, and make us obedient to Thy commands; through Jesus Christ our Lord[k].

6. *For a Blessing on Social Intercourse.*

O GOD, Who visitest the humble, and consolest us by the affection of our brethren; extend Thy grace to our fellowship, that by means of those in whom Thou dwellest, we may feel that Thou art come to visit us; through Jesus Christ our Lord[l].

[h] Leonine. [i] Ibid. [k] Gelasian.
[l] Gelasian. The Gregorian reading, "fraternâ *dilectione*," has been followed, instead of the Gelasian *dignatione*. Murat. i. 738; ii. 198.

O GOD, Who makest manifest to us in Thy servants the signs of Thine own Presence, send forth upon us the Spirit of love; that by the coming of our brethren and fellow-servants, Thy bountiful grace may be increased in ourselves; through Jesus Christ our Lord[m].

7. *Before and after Meals.*

BLESS, O Lord, Thy gifts, which we are about to receive from Thy bounty. May Thy gifts, O Lord, be our refreshment, and Thy grace our consolation; through our Lord[n].

WE have been satisfied, O Lord, with Thy gifts and bounties. Fill us with Thy mercy, Who art blessed, Who with the Father, &c.[o]

[m] Gelasian. [n] Ibid. [o] Ibid.

PRAYERS
FOR THE USE OF THE CLERGY.

1. *For Deacons.*

O LORD our God, Who by Thine own presence dost shed the abundance of Thy Holy Spirit on those who are set apart, by Thine inscrutable power, to become Ministers, and to serve Thy spotless Mysteries; keep Thy servant, whom Thou hast willed to be promoted to the ministry of a Deacon, that he may hold the mystery of the faith in a pure conscience, with all virtue; vouchsafe him the grace given to Thy first Martyr Stephen, who was first called by Thee to the work of this ministry; and enable him to administer according to Thy good pleasure the degree assigned to him by Thy goodness,—for they that minister rightly purchase to themselves a good degree;—and fill him, by the presence of Thy holy and life-giving Spirit, with all faith, and love, and power, and sanctification. For Thou art our God, and to Thee we render glory, Father, Son, and Holy Spirit, now and ever, and unto ages of ages[a].

[a] From two prayers in the Ordinal of the Eastern Church.

2. *For Priests.*

O GOD, great in power, unsearchable in understanding, wondrous in counsels towards the children of men, do Thou fill with the gift of the Holy Spirit him whom Thou hast willed to undertake the degree of the Priesthood; that he may be worthy to stand before Thy holy Altar unblameably, to announce the Gospel of Thy kingdom, to administer the Word of Thy truth, to offer gifts and spiritual Sacrifices unto Thee, and to renew Thy people in the laver of Regeneration; that at the second coming of our great God and Saviour Jesus Christ, Thine Only-begotten Son, he may go forth to meet Him, and by the multitude of Thy mercies receive his reward: for Thy venerable and majestic Name is blessed and glorified [b].

VERE dignum...Majestatem Tuam cunctis sensibus deprecari,...conservis cibaria ministrantes tempore competenti Dominico reperiamur adventu; famulosque Tuos cum dilectione corripere, et cum necessariâ studeamus amare censurâ; totumque servitium delegatum rationabiliter exsequentes, non reatum de neglecto Domini subeamus augmento, sed Divinorum nobis multiplicata proveniat dispensatio talentorum [c].

[b] Ordinal of the Eastern Church.

[c] Leon.

IT is meet for us to beseech Thy Majesty, that we may be found at our Lord's coming ministering to our fellow-servants their portion of meat in due season; that in our dealings with Thy servants we may be careful to join affection with rebuke, and needful censure with love; and that wisely discharging the service committed to us, we may not incur the guilt of neglecting to increase our Lord's deposit, but may receive profit from having multiplied God's talents, whereof we have been the stewards.

DA nobis, quæsumus, Omnipotens Deus, ut per gratiam Tuam nosmetipsos, sicut Te dignum est, exhibentes, Tuis fidelibus ministremus rectæ conversationis exemplum; et populi Tui salvatio sempiterna fiat præmium sacerdotis; per, &c.[d]

GRANT to us, we beseech Thee, Almighty God, that we may so behave ourselves by Thy grace as to be worthy of Thee, and may afford to Thy faithful people the example of a right conversation; and that the everlasting salvation of Thy people may become the reward of the priest; through our Lord.

DEUS mundi Creator et Rector, ad humilitatis meæ preces placatus attende; et me famulum

[d] Leon.

Tuum, quem nullis suffragantibus meritis, sed immensæ largitate clementiæ, cœlestibus Mysteriis servire tribuisti, dignum sacris altaribus fac ministrum[e].

O GOD, the Creator and Ruler of the world, favourably give heed to the prayers which I humbly offer; and as Thou hast granted me, Thy servant, not on the ground of any desert of mine, but out of the bounty of Thine infinite goodness, to serve the heavenly Mysteries, so make me a worthy minister of Thy sacred altar; through Jesus Christ our Lord.

DOMINE sancte, Pater omnipotens, æterne Deus, gratiæ Tuæ in nobis dona prosequere; et quod possibilitas non habet fragilitatis humanæ, Tuo Spiritu miseratus impende; ut sacris altaribus servientes et fidei integritate fundati, et mentis sint claritate conspicui. Per, &c.[f]

O HOLY Lord, Father Almighty, everlasting God, carry onward in us the gifts of Thy grace; and mercifully bestow by Thy Spirit what human frailty cannot attain; that they who attend at the sacred altars may be both grounded in perfect faith, and conspicuous by the brightness of their souls; through Jesus Christ our Lord.

[e] Leon. [f] Ibid. See p. 102.

QUIS hoc dignus exsistat officio, nisi gratiâ Tuæ miserationis præventus aptetur? Quum ergo Tui doni, non nostri sit meriti, Tuæ nihilominus gubernationis intererit, ut non sit negligentibus pœna perpetua, sed potius exsequentibus competenter fiat causa remunerationis æternæ [g].

WHO can be worthy of this office, unless he is first fitted for it by Thy preventing grace and compassion? Since then it is of Thy gift, not of our merit, Thou must also interpose Thy guidance, that it may not prove the everlasting punishment of our negligence, but rather become in due order the cause of an eternal reward for our having discharged it; through Jesus Christ our Lord.

ECCLESIAM Tuam, Domine, benignus illustra; ut et gregis Tui proficiat ubique successus, et grati fiant Nomini Tuo, Te gubernante, pastores. Per, &c.[h]

GRACIOUSLY cast Thy light, O Lord, upon Thy Church; that Thy flock may everywhere go on and prosper, and its pastors, by Thy governance, may become acceptable to Thy Name; through Jesus Christ our Lord.

[g] Leon. [h] Ibid.

DEUS misericors, Rex æterne, da servituti nostræ prosperum cursum: et ut Tibi in populi Tui devotione placeamus, Tu sancto præside gregi, et ad Tuorum observantiam mandatorum Tu omnium dirige voluntates[i].

O MERCIFUL God and eternal King, give a prosperous course to our service; and that we may become pleasing in Thy sight by means of the devotion of Thy people, do Thou preside over Thy holy flock; and guide Thou the wills of all into the observance of Thy commands.

MISERICORS et miserator Domine, Qui nos parcendo sustentas, et ignoscendo sanctificas, da veniam peccatis nostris, et Sacramentis cœlestibus servientes ab omni culpâ liberos esse concede. Per, &c.[k]

O MERCIFUL and pitying Lord, Who supportest us by sparing us, and sanctifiest us by forgiving; vouchsafe pardon to our sins, and grant that those who attend on the heavenly Sacraments may be free from all offence, through Jesus Christ our Lord.

DEUS, Qui populis Tuis indulgentiâ consulis, et amore dominaris; da Spiritum sapientiæ quibus dedisti regimen disciplinæ; ut de profectu

i Leon. k Gelas.

sanctarum ovium fiant gaudia æterna pastorum. Per, &c.[l]

O GOD, Who providest for Thy people with tenderness, and rulest over them in love; give the Spirit of wisdom to those to whom Thou hast given the authority of government; that from the well-being of the holy sheep may proceed the eternal joy of the pastors; through Jesus Christ our Lord.

FAC me, quæso, Omnipotens Deus, ita justitiâ indui, ut in Sanctorum Tuorum merear exsultatione lætari; quatenus emundatus ab omnibus sordibus peccatorum, consortium adipiscar Tibi placentium Sacerdotum; meque Tua misericordia à vitiis omnibus exuat, quem reatus propriæ conscientiæ gravat. Per, &c.[m]

MAKE me, I beseech Thee, Almighty God, to be so arrayed in righteousness, that I may be enabled to rejoice in the gladness of Thy Saints; so that being cleansed from all filthiness of sin, I may attain the fellowship of the Priests who are pleasing unto Thee; and that I, who am burdened by the guilt of my own conscience, may be delivered by Thy mercy from all vices; through our Lord Jesus Christ.

[l] Gregor. [m] Ibid.

DEUS, Qui dissimulatis humanæ fragilitatis peccatis, Sacerdotii dignitatem concedis indignis; et non solum peccata dimittis, verum etiam ipsos peccatores justificare dignaris; Cujus est muneris ut non exsistentia sumant exordia, exorta nutrimentum, nutrita fructum, fructuosa perseverandi auxilium; Qui me non exsistentem creasti, creatum fidei firmitate ditasti, fidelem, quamvis peccatis squalentem, Sacerdotii dignitate donasti; Tuam omnipotentiam supplex exposco, ut me a præteritis peccatis emacules, in mundi hujus cursu à bonis operibus corrobores, et in perseverantiæ soliditate confirmes. Sicque me facias Tuis altaribus deservire, ut ad eorum qui Tibi placuerunt Sacerdotum consortium valeam pervenire: et per Eum Tibi sit meum acceptabile votum, Qui Se Tibi obtulit in Sacrificium, Qui est omnium Opifex, et solus sine peccati maculâ Pontifex, Jesus Christus Dominus noster[n].

O GOD, Who, passing over the sins of human frailty, dost vouchsafe to unworthy men the dignity of the Priesthood; and not only pardonest sins, but also art pleased to justify the sinners themselves; of Whose gift it cometh that things which are not should receive a beginning,—having begun, should receive nourishment,—being nou-

[n] Gregor.

rished, should bear fruit,—and being fruitful, should be aided to continue; Who hast created me when I was not,—having created me, hast endued me with stedfast faith, and given to me, being one of the faithful, although defiled by sin, the dignity of the Priesthood; I humbly beseech Thine Almighty goodness to cleanse me from my past sins, to strengthen me in good works during my passage through this world, and to confirm me in unwavering perseverance. And make me so to serve Thine altars, that I may be able to attain the fellowship of those priests who have been pleasing unto Thee. And may my prayer be acceptable to Thee through Him Who offered up Himself to Thee as a Sacrifice, Who is the Maker of all things, and the only High Priest without spot of sin, Jesus Christ our Lord.

3. *Celebration of the Holy Eucharist* [o].

DEUS, Fons bonitatis, et pietatis Origo, Qui peccantem non statim judicas, sed ad pœnitentiam miseratus exspectas; Te quæso ut facinorum meorum squalores abstergas, et me ad peragendum injunctum officium dignum efficias; et qui altaris Tui ministerium suscepi indignus, perago trepidus, ad id peragendum reddar strenuus, et inter eos qui Tibi placuerunt inveniar justificatus. Per, &c. [p]

[o] These prayers may be added by a celebrant to some of those provided above for communicants.

[p] Gregor.

O GOD, the Fountain of goodness, and Source of kindness, Who dost not straightway condemn the sinner, but compassionately waitest for his repentance; I pray Thee to wipe away the foulness of my offences, and make me meet to perform the office laid upon me; and that I who have unworthily undertaken, and tremblingly execute, the ministration of Thine altar, may be rendered strong to perform it, and be found justified among those who have pleased Thee; through Jesus Christ our Lord.

AURES Tuæ pietatis, mitissime Deus, inclina precibus meis, et gratiâ Sancti Spiritûs illumina cor meum; ut Tuis Mysteriis dignè ministrare, Teque æternâ caritate diligere, et sempiterna gaudia percipere merear. Per Christum[q].

O MOST merciful God, incline Thy loving ears to my prayers, and illuminate my heart with the grace of the Holy Spirit, that I may be enabled worthily to minister to Thy Mysteries, and to love Thee with an everlasting love, and to attain everlasting joys, through Jesus Christ our Lord[r].

WE give Thee thanks, O Lord God of hosts, Who hast counted us worthy even now to

[q] Miss. Ebor.
[r] This beautiful Collect of the Ordinarium Missæ, in the Use of York, is enlarged from a Gallican collect of Charlemagne's time, in Martene, i. 518. See also Menard, p. 266.

stand at Thy holy Altar, and to entreat Thy compassion for our sins and for the errors of Thy people. Accept, O Lord, our supplication; make us worthy to offer unto Thee supplications and prayers and bloodless sacrifices for all Thy people; and enable us, whom Thou hast placed in this ministry, by the power of Thy Holy Spirit, without condemnation and without offence, and keeping the witness of our conscience pure, to call upon Thee in every time and place [s].

DOMINE Deus, Omnipotens Pater, benedic et sanctifica hoc sacrificium laudis [t], quod Tibi oblatum est ad honorem et gloriam Nominis Tui; et parce peccatis populi Tui, et exaudi orationem meam, et dimitte mihi omnia peccata mea. Per Christum Dominum nostrum [u].

O LORD God, Father Almighty, bless and sanctify this sacrifice of praise, which has been offered unto Thee, to the honour and glory of Thy Name; and pardon the sins of Thy people, and hear

[s] Liturgy of S. Chrysostom. "The first prayer of the Faithful after the unfolding of the corporal."

[t] Meaning the elements. So in the Roman Canon, as S. Leo used it, "hoc sacrificium laudis" is equivalent to "hæc dona, hæc munera, hæc sancta sacrificia illibata." Compare Leonine, Mur. i. 419, "Ad altaria veneranda cum hostiis laudis accedimus;" and i. 380, "Hostias Tibi, Domine, laudis offerimus." So Gelasian, Mur. i. 599; and in a Gregorian *Super oblata*, Mur. ii. 196, "hoc sacrificium laudis" is synonymous with "hæc sancta." Compare the phrases, "spiritalis hostia," "rationalis hostia," "nostræ devotionis oblatio," Mur. ii. 691, 654, i. 527; all referring, like the Eastern phrase, "reasonable and unbloody service," to the elements.

[u] Miss. Mozarab.

my prayer, and forgive me all my sins; through Christ our Lord.

ATTEND, O Lord Jesus Christ our God, from Thy holy habitation, and from the glorious throne of Thy kingdom, and come to sanctify us, Thou Who sittest above with the Father, and art here invisibly present with us; vouchsafe with Thy mighty hand to impart Thine immaculate Body and Thy precious Blood to us, and by us to all Thy people[x].

MUNERUM Tuorum, Domine, largitate gaudentes, supplices deprecamur, ut quibus donasti hujus ministerii facultatem, tribuas sufficientem gratiam ministrandi. Per, &c.[y]

REJOICING, O Lord, in the richness of Thy gifts, we humbly pray that as Thou hast given us power to hold this ministry, so Thou wilt give us sufficient grace to fulfil it; through our Lord.

HUJUS, Domine, perceptio Sacramenti peccatorum meorum maculas tergat, et ad peragendum injunctum officium me idoneum reddat. Per, &c.[z]

MAY the reception of this Sacrament, O Lord, efface the stains of my sins, and render me

[x] Liturgy of S. Chrysostom. [y] Leon. [z] Gregor.

capable of the discharge of the office laid upon me; through our Lord.

PROCEEDING from strength to strength, and having finished the Divine Liturgy in Thy temple, we now entreat Thee, Lord our God, vouchsafe us to enjoy Thy perfect love[a].

4. *Baptism and other Ordinances.*

DEUS, Qui invisibili potentiâ Tuâ Sacramentorum Tuorum mirabiliter operaris effectum, et licet nos tantis mysteriis exsequendis simus indigni, Tu tamen gratiæ Tuæ dona non deseris, etiam ad nostras preces aures Tuæ pietatis inclina.—Nobis præcepta servantibus Tu, Deus Omnipotens, clemens adesto, Tu benignus adspira[b].

O GOD, Who, by Thine invisible power, dost wonderfully work out the effect of Thy Sacraments, and although we be unworthy to perform such great mysteries, yet Thou forsakest not the gifts of Thy grace, incline Thy gracious ears even to our entreaty; be present to us in Thy goodness, assist us in Thy loving-kindness, while we are observing Thy commands, O God Almighty.

QUOD humilitatis nostræ gerendum est ministerio, Tuæ virtutis compleatur effectu[c].

[a] Liturgy of S. James.
[b] Gelas. Part of the Consecration of the Font on Easter Eve.
[c] Gelas.

MAY that which is to be performed by our humble ministration, be fulfilled by Thine effectual power.

ADESTO, Domine, supplicationibus nostris; et me, qui etiam misericordiâ Tuâ primus indigeo, clementer exaudi; et quem non electione meriti, sed dono gratiæ Tuæ, constituisti hujus operis ministrum, da fiduciam Tui muneris exsequendi, et Ipse in nostro ministerio quod Tuæ pietatis est operare. Per, &c.[d]

BE present, O Lord, to our supplications; and graciously hearken unto me, who am the first to need Thy mercy; and as Thou hast made me the minister of this work, not by choosing me on account of merit, but by the gift of Thy grace, so give me confidence to perform Thine office, and do Thou Thyself by our ministration carry out the act of Thine own loving-kindness; through our Lord.

ADESTO, misericors Deus, ut quod actum est nostræ servitutis officio Tuâ benedictione firmetur. Per, &c.[e]

BE present, O merciful God; that what has been done by our office and service may be confirmed by Thy benediction; through our Lord.

[d] Gelas. A prayer said over penitents on Maundy Thursday.
[e] Leon.

5. *Preaching.*

OMNIPOTENS sempiterne Deus, Origo cunctarum et Perfectio virtutum; da nobis, quæsumus, et exercere quæ recta sunt, et prædicare quæ vera; ut instructionem gratiæ Tuæ præbeamus et agendo Tuis fidelibus et docendo. Per, &c.[f]

ALMIGHTY and everlasting God, the Source and Perfection of all virtues; grant us, we beseech Thee, both to do what is right and to preach what is true; that both by action and teaching we may afford to Thy faithful people the instruction which is of Thy grace; through Jesus Christ our Lord.

6. *Visitation*[g].

EXAUDI nos, Domine sancte, Pater omnipotens, æterne Deus, et humilitatis nostræ officiis gratiam[h] Tuæ visitationis admisce; ut quorum adimus habitacula, Tu in eorum Tibi cordibus facias mansionem. Per, &c.[i]

HEAR us, holy Lord, Father Almighty, everlasting God, and join the grace of Thine own visitation to our humble services; that Thou mayest make Thyself a mansion in the hearts of those

[f] Leon. [g] See also the Intercessions for a Family.
[h] *Gratiæ*, in the text, is clearly corrupt. [i] Gelas.

whose dwelling we approach; through Jesus Christ our Lord.

PROTECTOR fidelium Deus, et subditarum Tibi mentium Frequentator, habitantibus in hac domo famulis Tuis propitius adesse digneris; ut quos nos humanâ visitamus sollicitudine, Tu divinâ munias potestate. Per, &c.[k]

O GOD, the Protector of the faithful, and constant Visitor of souls obedient unto Thee; may it please Thee to be present, with Thy favour, to Thy servants who dwell in this house; that while we visit them with human solicitude, Thou mayest guard them with Divine favour; through our Lord.

BENEDIC, Domine, hanc domum et omnes habitantes in eâ, sicut benedicere dignatus es domum Abraham, Isaac et Jacob; ut in his parietibus Angelus lucis inhabitet, sentiant in eâ commorantes rore cœli abundantiam[l], et per indulgentiam lætentur pacifici et securi[m].

BLESS, O Lord, this house and all who dwell in it, as Thou wast pleased to bless the house of Abraham, Isaac, and Jacob, that within these walls may dwell an Angel of light, and that those

[k] Gelas. [l] See Vulg., Gen. xxvii. 28,—"Det tibi Deus de rore cœli . . . abundantiam," &c. [m] Gelas.

who dwell together in it may receive the abundant dew of heavenly blessing, and through Thy tenderness rejoice in peace and quiet; through Jesus Christ our Lord.

OMNIPOTENS et misericors Deus, Qui sacerdotum ministerio ad Tibi serviendum et supplicandum uti dignaris; quæsumus immensam clementiam Tuam, ut quidquid modo visitamus visites, quidquid benedicimus benedicas, sitque ad nostræ humilitatis introitum[n]...fuga dæmonum, Angeli pacis ingressus. Per, &c.[o]

ALMIGHTY and merciful God, Who art pleased to use the ministry of priests for the rendering of service and prayer to Thee; we implore Thy boundless mercy, that whatever we now visit Thou wouldest visit, whatever we bless Thou wouldest bless, and that at Thy humble servants' entrance evil spirits may flee away, and the Angel of peace may come in; through Jesus Christ our Lord.

OMNIPOTENS et misericors Deus, quæsumus immensam pietatem Tuam, ut ad introitum humilitatis nostræ hunc famulum Tuum *illum* in hoc tabernaculo fessum jacentem salutiferè visitare digneris[p].

[n] A few words are here omitted. [o] Gregor.
[p] From a Rheims manuscript Ritual cited by Menard.

ALMIGHTY and merciful God, we beseech Thy boundless loving-kindness, that at Thy humble servants' entrance Thou wouldest be pleased to visit with Thy salvation this Thy servant *N.* who is lying, worn with sickness, in this house.

MAY the Father bless thee, Who created all things in the beginning; May the Son of God heal thee; May the Holy Ghost enlighten thee, guard thy body, save thy soul, direct thy thoughts, and bring thee safe to the heavenly country; Who liveth and reigneth God, in a perfect Trinity, throughout all ages[r].

OUR Lord Jesus Christ be near thee to defend thee, within thee to refresh thee, around thee to preserve thee, before thee to guide thee, behind thee to justify thee, above thee to bless thee; Who liveth and reigneth, &c.[s]

7. *Anniversary of Ordination*[t].

DEUS, Cujus arbitrio omnium sæculorum ordo decurrit; respice propitius ad me famulum Tuum, quem ad ordinem Presbyterii[u] promovere

[r] Sarum.
[s] From a manuscript Ritual of the tenth century cited by Menard.
[t] See Heygate's *Probatio Clerica*, p. 83. "By no means forget the day of your Ordination,' &c.
[u] The Sacramentaries use *Sacerdos* as a title of both *Episcopus* and *Presbyter*. In this same Mass, Mur. i. 712, we find, "Quam Tibi offero famulus Tuus et sacerdos, pro eo quod me eligere dignatus es in ordinem presbyterii."

dignatus es; et ut Tibi mea servitus placeat, Tua in me misericorditer dona conserva. Per, &c. [v]

O GOD, by Whose command the order of all time runs its course; look graciously upon me Thy servant, whom Thou hast been pleased to promote to the order of the Presbyterate; and that my service may be pleasing unto Thee, do Thou mercifully preserve in me Thy gifts; through Jesus Christ our Lord.

8. *Prayer for the Flock.*

QUIA non mihi alibi est fiducia, nisi in misericordiâ Tuâ, Tu et os meum præconio veritatis perenna, et opus pleniori ubertate sanctifica; ut et indignum me salves, et commissum mihi gregem pro Tuâ pietate justifices. Quidquid in illis vitiatum respicis, sana; quidquid in me vitiosum inspicis, cura. Si quam vitio tepiditatis meæ vel incuriâ contraxerunt vel contrahunt labem, omitte. Si quo etiam me ignorante, vel cognito [x], deciderunt in crimine, atque si exempli mei offendiculo proruerunt, ignosce, et pro culpis talibus misero mihi ultionis non restituas vicem. His tamen quibus increpationis visus sum adhibere [y] judicium, et increpatio ipsa eis proficiat ad salutem, et oratio hæc interpellans commisso eos revocet ab errore, ut non perferant tartareos cruciatus;—quo illo-

[v] Gelas. [x] Menard proposes *cognoscente*. [y] Probably "adhibendo."

rum iniquitatibus tribuas veniam, et meam abluas contractam de regendi incommoditate offensam. Præbe, Deus, aurem sacrificiis nostris, et me mihique commissos Tuis adscribe in paginis; quo cum grege mihi credito, et a cuncto eluar crimine, et ad Te merear pervenire in pace[1].

SEEING that I have no confidence in anything but Thy mercy, do Thou endue my mouth with power to proclaim Thy truth, and sanctify my work with more abundant richness of grace, that Thou mayest both save my unworthy self, and justify in Thy loving-kindness the flock entrusted to me. Whatever Thou seest corrupt in them, do Thou make sound; and whatever Thou discernest vicious in me, do Thou cure; whatever guilt they have contracted or do contract, through my sinful lukewarmness or carelessness, do Thou put away. If in anything they have fallen into sin, whether with or without my knowledge, or have fallen by the stumblingblock of my example, pardon them, and render not to my unhappy self the punishment which such a fault deserves. But let the rebukes which I have administered in censure of others conduce to their salvation; and let the pleading of this prayer recall them from the error they have committed, that they may not endure the torments

[1] From an "Apologia Sacerdotis" in Menard's Gregorian.

of hell:—so that Thou mayest vouchsafe pardon to their iniquities, and wash away the offence of which I have become guilty by my own unfitness to bear rule. Incline Thine ear, O God, to our sacrifices, and write me, and those who are committed to me, in Thy books; whereby, together with the flock entrusted to me, I may both be cleansed from all sin, and be enabled to attain to Thee in peace.

RESPICE de cœlo, Christe, super gregem et agnos Tuos,—et benedic corpora et animas eorum.—Qui signum Tuum, Christe, in frontibus eorum acceperunt, Tuos esse concedas in die judicii[a].

LOOK down from heaven, O Christ, on Thy flock and lambs, and bless their bodies and souls. Grant those who have received Thy sign, O Christ, on their foreheads, to be Thine own in the day of judgment.

[a] Pontif. Egb.

APPENDIX.

ON

THE COLLECTS IN THE PRAYER-BOOK.

IT may be well to add to the above series of translations a few remarks on the subject of Collects in general, and, in particular, of those which form so important an element in the English Ritual.

It would be easy to draw up a series of extracts from various writers, bearing witness to the majesty and the preciousness of our Anglican Collects. In such a *catena*, the popular historian who has spoken of the "beautiful Collects, which have soothed the griefs of forty generations of Christians," and who has pointed a quiet sarcasm at the Commissioners of 1689, for their tasteless resolution that Patrick should make the Collects longer, by way of making them more affecting, would be united with Bishop Sanderson, who pronounced them to be "the most passionate, proper, and most elegant comprehensive expressions that any language ever afforded;" with the gifted Irish layman, who said that for 1200 years they had been as the manna in the wilderness to devout spirits, and were, next to Scripture itself, the clearest standards whereby genuine piety might be discerned; and with divines of our own day, who dwell on the stores of exact theology which are laid up in the Collects, and on their power to deliver our worship from incoherency, and to sustain it with "strong and satisfying views" of the Divine love[a].

It is, indeed, this wonderful blending of strength and sweetness in the Collects, which has called forth so much love and admiration, and has made them such a bond of union for pious minds of different times and countries; even as the same imagery, in regard to their effect, naturally occurs to a bishop of Treves in the sixth century, and to an Anglican poet in the nineteenth. Martene[b] quotes the words of S. Nicetius,—"et psalmis delectamur, et orationibus *irrigamur*;" and the author of the "Cathedral" likens the thoughts which the Sunday Collect brings to—

"healthful founts in Elim green,
Casting a freshness o'er the week."

Nor is it a small advantage which the Collect-type of prayer secures to any community that adopts it, that it answers the end which, as Hooker,

[a] Macaulay, Hist. Eng., i. 160; iii. 476: Walton's Life of Sanderson: Alex. Knox's Remains, ii. 357: Trench—Star of the Wise Men, p. 73; Synonyms of New Test., p. 73: Maurice on the Prayer-book, p. 173.
[b] De Aut. Eccl. Rit. iii. 50.

quoting S. Augustine, tells us, the Egyptian monks proposed to themselves—namely, to preserve "that vigilant and erect attention of mind, which in prayer is very necessary, from being wasted or dulled through continuance, if their prayers were few or long:" for which purpose,—or, as Cassian expressed it, "both to solicit God more earnestly by frequent addresses, and to avoid the temptations of Satan drawing them into lassitude and weariness,"—they resolved that their prayers should be many and brief, like darts cast forth with energy [c]. This is doubtless chiefly realized by *preces* and ejaculations; but also to a considerable extent by Collects, especially when compared with such wordy effusions as exist in Knox's "Book of Common Order."

Thus it is that many persons, not by any means predisposed in favour of ancient formularies, will often be attracted (if they are free from Puritanic prejudice) by prayers which say so much in saying so little; which address the Most High with such adoring awe, and utter man's needs with such profound pathos, yet with such a calm intensity—assailing "Heaven's door," as our great Church poet says [d], with the "forceful knocking" of determined faith; which are perpetually insisting on the abso-

[c] S. Aug. Ep. 130: Hooker, b. v. c. 33: Bingham, b. xiv. c. 1, s. 7.
[d] Lyra Innocentium, p. 247, 1st ed.

lute necessity of Grace, the Fatherly tenderness of God, the might of the all-prevailing Name; which are never weak, never diluted, never drawling, never ill-arranged, never a provocation to listlessness; which exhibit an exquisite skill of antithesis, and a rhythmical harmony which the ear is loth to lose. They do indeed adapt themselves, as Mr. Maurice expresses it, "with a marvellous flexibility, to all the different conditions of the human spirit;" and thus admit of a rich variety of construction, subject to a general law of threefold division, which Mr. Freeman has well stated*:—

1. Introduction.—Invocation of God's Name; often, but not always, including a commemoration of one of His attributes, or of one of His actions.
2. Main part.—Petition for some boon, often, but not always, accompanied by a statement of the good to be expected from such boon.
3. Conclusion.—Glory given to God, or affiance in Christ, or both together.

The petition is often twofold: as in the Fourteenth Collect after Trinity, which is one of the oldest we have, and in which are two distinct sentences of supplication; or in the Third after Easter, which is of the same date, and has one supplication branching out into two clauses. In some cases, as

* Principles of Divine Service i. 372.

in the First after Trinity, the petition is prefaced by a statement of the need which excites it. So, too, the statement of the good result is often richly amplified; as in the Fourth after Easter, and the Fourth after Trinity, and that beautiful Collect for the Annunciation, which was so manifestly intended to keep Lenten thoughts and the coming joys of Easter in combination with the gratitude for God's first assumption of our flesh.

The general rule is, that a Collect is addressed to God the Father. Pope Benedict XIV. quotes Cardinal Bona's statement, that only a few Collects are expressly offered to the Son, and none to the Holy Spirit[f]; partly because the Eucharistic worship has regard to the Sacrifice offered to the Father by the Son. It is observable that the Collect for the Fourth Sunday in Advent, which in the Gelasian Sacramentary addresses the Father, in the Gregorian is more happily transferred to the Son; in our version it has resumed its old form. And now the three Collects which in our Prayer-book address the Son are—S. Stephen's, originally addressed to the Father; Third in Advent, and First in Lent, which were composed respectively in 1661 and 1549. It is strange that when the revisers took up

[f] In the Mozarabic rite some Collects are addressed to the Holy Spirit. See Miss. Moz. 258, 263. On Whitsunday, indeed, in this rite, the "great oblation" itself is addressed to Him. This was probably, in its origin, a protest against Arianism, which was dominant in Spain until 589.

the old Vesper Antiphon of the Ascension, which flowed from the dying lips of Bede [g], and turned it into a Collect for the Sunday after Ascension, they should not have retained its ancient character as an appeal to the Son, the ascended King of glory. The Trinity Collect, in its oldest form, was an address to the Father, through our Lord; but Mr. Maskell [h] says that the mediæval English Church used it as a prayer to the whole Trinity.

The question of the etymology of the "Collect" has produced a variety of theories. We may derive it (1) from the circumstances of those who use the prayer, or else (2) from something in the nature of the prayer itself. In the former case, it may be derived from the *collecta*, or "assembly for worship," (Mr. Freeman would say, for *non*-eucharistic worship,) as Alcuin thought, and as is implied in an old book of devotion cited by Mr. Maskell, "The Mirrour of Our Lady," which explained a Collect to mean a prayer of persons who are gathered together in unity, as representing Holy Church; or it may be traced to the *collectedness* and concentration of mind required in the worshippers. Both these views are mentioned by Pope Benedict XIV. and by Gavanti [i].

[g] "O Rex gloriæ, Domine virtutum, Qui triumphator hodie super omnes cœlos ascendisti, ne derelinquas nos orphanos, sed mitte promissum Patris in nos, Spiritum Veritatis. Alleluia." At the "forsake us not," he burst into tears.

[h] Monum. Rit. ii. 28.

[i] De S. Miss. Sacrif. ii. c. 5; Thesaur. S. Rit., tom. i. p. 53.

In the latter case, there are two main views:—

First, that which considers the Collect as a condensed form of certain *Scriptural* teaching,—the substance of a certain quantity of God's Word. And this theory is often more precisely stated, by the derivation of the word "Collect" from the circumstance that in many cases it is the quintessence of the practical lessons deducible from the Epistle and Gospel for the day. Wheatly prefers this view for the *Communion* Collect; and Mr. Freeman has made it very attractive, by his learned and skilful advocacy[j]. The *oratio*, as said at the Holy Communion, and as transferred into the Morning Office, he explains on this principle; not so, of course, any other use of the *oratio* or Collect. The Dean of Westminster, in his "Study of Words," adopts this view; and similarly in his "Star of the Wise Men," he describes the word as meaning a collection of the Church's thoughts in regard to the day[k].

Secondly, that which considers the thing collected to be *prayer*. Pope Benedict gives this as the first of three views which he mentions:—"Quia sacerdos, qui veluti mediator est inter Deum et homines, *vota omnium colligit.*" "In that one prayer," says Mr. Maskell, "*many were collected*

[j] Principles of Divine Service, i. 6, 146, 212, 367.
[k] Trench's Study of Words, p. 209; Star of the Wise Men, p. 72.

together[l]." It is not at all necessary, in support of this view, to maintain—what would not be borne out by the Leonine Sacramentary—that the oldest rituals prescribe only one Missal Collect; although it may be, that where more than one are appointed, yet one of them is *the* Collect *par excellence*. But if there were two or three, each might be said to gather up and consolidate, in a few words, the devotional aspirations of the people. It is singular that in the ancient rites of S. John Lateran no Collect at all, save the Lord's Prayer, was ordinarily said at Matins and Vespers; the "mother and head" of Western Churches being supposed to assert its own pre-eminence by this adherence to "the sum of all prayer." But even in its Daily Office there were some Collects which were said by the Pope, or by any of "his seven collateral Bishops;" and its Eucharistic practice did not differ in regard to Collects from that of other Churches[m], although it was supposed to have done so by Durandus, Pope Benedict, and Martene.

There is a special application of the view now before us to the Collect as said at the end of the Daily Offices. After the main portion of the service was over, it was usual for the chief of the

[l] Anc. Lit., p. 30.

[m] See Azevedo's edition of the Lateran Missal, Rome, 1754. In his preface (p. xxxii. sq.) he shows that Durandus misunderstood his authority, John the Deacon, who did not say that the Lateran had no Collect at Mass, but that it had none in the Offices.

clergy present, if there were more than one, or for the minister officiating, in other cases, to "collect the prayer," *colligere orationem;* that is, to offer a short prayer by which the previous worship was summed up and recommended to God. With this, in many cases, the office of that hour concluded. Bishop Sparrow, Bingham, and Lingard lay stress on this fact[n]. But it cannot be taken as explaining all the phenomena of the Collect; for, not to say that the Communion Collect does not come at the end of a series of devotions, these *orationes collectæ*, or *collectæ* simply, were in some monastic rules offered before the concluding part of the service; S. Cæsarius of Arles bade his monks to insert them between the Lessons; and they were sometimes said at the end of the Psalms[o]. If, then, we determine to adopt the etymology of the gathering up of *prayer* as the general account of the Collect, (instead of referring one kind of Collect to this origin, another to that, which does, indeed, present a difficulty,) we must forbear to dwell on the use of such a prayer at the *end* of a service, and must say generally that it is an *oratio*, as it was usually called in Rome and Spain,—an *orison*, to use the old English term,—in which many elements of supplication meet, and many devout thoughts

[n] Rationale, p. 64: Antiq., b. xv. c. 1, s. 2: Anglo-Sax. Ch. i. 297.
[o] See Martene, iv. 16, 33, 34.

present themselves. In this sense we might borrow the language of a beautiful passage in Mr. Freeman's book, and speak of the West as "*comprehending all the spiritual needs of man in Collects of matchless profundity*[p]."

And doubtless the Collect-form, as we have it, is Western in every feature; in that "unity of sentiment and severity of style" which Lord Macaulay[q] has admired; in its Roman brevity and majestic conciseness, its freedom from all luxuriant ornament and all inflation of phraseology. It has a truly illustrious Roman parentage; its inventor, Mr. Freeman says, was S. Leo[r], emphatically and justly named the Great, who held the first see of Christendom from 440 to 461. Of him it may be said, even by those who cannot shut their eyes "to his ambition and love of domination[s]," that although by human weakness he was led to grasp at excessive authority, and, so far, left an evil example to his successors, yet by faith he confronted Attila and Genseric with a dignity which compelled their reverence; by faith he so proclaimed the One Christ in Two Natures as well-nigh to justify the famous acclamation, "Peter hath spoken by Leo;" by faith he stood forth as the first great Roman preacher, in sermons full

[p] Princ. of Div. Serv. i. 274.
[q] Essay on Milton.
[r] Gavanti names Ambrose.
[s] Robertson, Ch. Hist. i. 443.

of Christ; by faith he maintained religion "on the throne of Rome alone, of all the greater sees, in its majesty, its sanctity, its piety[t]."

Taking, then, the view that Leo was the main constructor of the Collect-type of prayers, we may consider to what extent our present series of Church Collects is indebted to his compositions. The fragment of a Sacramentary, attributed to him, is supposed by Muratori to be his in a certain sense; that is, to be a series of *missæ* containing much that he wrote[u], but also some passages which may be referred to his predecessors, and some which belong to his immediate successors; the whole being put together, by a not very skilful hand, under the pontificate of Felix, commonly called the Third, who sate from 483 to 492. Muratori calls it a most precious monument of antiquity, unparalleled in its kind, as exhibiting the *ancient* Roman service, and containing a rich store of ecclesiastical knowledge. "Monendus est lector," he observes in conclusion, "quamquam de auctore pretiosi hujus, atque omnium antiquissimi Sacramentarii nihil certè habeamus, posse illud tamen, jam editum à Patre Blanchinio, *Sancti Leonis Magni* nomen retinere[x]."

[t] Milman, Lat. Christ. i. 178.

[u] E. g. compare Murat. i. 319, 322, with Leo, Serm. 78, on the Fast after Pentecost.

[x] Murat. i. 37. Mone considers the collection to be the work of a private person, a contemporary of Leo.

It will be worth while to give the originals of the Collects which we derive ultimately from this work.

1. *Third Sunday after Easter.* Leonine, in twentieth Mass for April, Mur. i. 301. This Collect clearly refers to the condition of those who had been baptized on Easter Eve:—

"Deus, Qui errantibus, ut in viam possint redire, veritatis lumen ostendis; da cunctis qui Christianâ professione censentur, et illa respuere quæ huic inimica sunt nomini, et ea quæ sunt apta sectari. Per." &c.

The words, "of righteousness," seem to have been added by S. Gregory.

2. *Fifth Sunday after Trinity.* Leonine, among Masses for July, Mur. i. 379. It seems to have been suggested, like several others in the Leonine, by the disasters of the dying Western Empire:—

"Da nobis, Domine Deus noster, ut et mundi cursus pacificè nobis Tuo ordine dirigatur, et Ecclesia Tua tranquillâ devotione lætetur. Per," &c.

3. *Ninth Sunday after Trinity.* Leonine, among Masses for September, Mur. i. 434:—

"Largire nobis, Domine, quæsumus, spiritum cogitandi quæ bona sunt *promptius* et agendi, ut qui sine Te esse non possumus, secundum Te vivere valeamus. Per," &c.

4. *Thirteenth Sunday after Trinity.* Leonine, for July, Mur. i. 371:—

"Omnipotens et misericors Deus, de Cujus munere venit, ut Tibi à fidelibus Tuis dignè et laudabiliter serviatur; tribue ut ad promissiones Tuas sine offensione curramus. Per," &c.

5. *Fourteenth Sunday after Trinity.* Leonine, for July, Mur. i. 374:—

"Omnipotens sempiterne Deus, da nobis fidei, spei, et caritatis augmentum; et ut mereamur assequi quod promittis, fac nos amare quod præcipis. Per," &c.

To these may be added the following Collects, as containing the substance of our Collects for the Tenth and Twelfth Sundays after Trinity. A translation of the first has been given among the Introductory Prayers:—

"Ad aures misericordiæ Tuæ, Domine, supplicum vota perveniant; et ut possimus impetrare quæ poscimus, fac nos semper Tibi placita postulare. Per," &c.[y]

"Virtutum cœlestium Deus, Qui plura præstas quam petimus aut meremur; tribue, quæsumus, ut Tuâ nobis misericordiâ conferatur, quod nostrorum non habet fiducia meritorum. Per," &c.[z]

The Sacramentary ascribed to S. Gelasius, Bishop of Rome from 492 to 496, was published at Rome,

[y] Mur. i. 381. [z] Ibid., 418.

in 1680, by Thomasius, afterwards Cardinal, from a manuscript belonging to the Queen of Sweden, which had been seen by Morinus and Bona. Muratori entertains no doubt that it is substantially the work of Gelasius, although (like the Gregorian Sacramentary) its text contains additions of later times. It is known that this Pontiff wrote Collects and Prefaces, (he is also said to have composed hymns in the Ambrosian manner,) and it may be safely affirmed that he digested the existing collection of Communion Collects, Prefaces, and other prayers,—not, of course, including the order of the daily offices,—into a new system, adding much that was original. It is interesting to regard Gelasius on this devotional side of his character, since we know from other evidence what he was as a theologian and a Church ruler: how zealous against Nestorians and Monophysites; how emphatic in maintaining the Real Presence, together with the permanence of the nature of the Bread and Wine[a]; how earnest against the "sacrilegious division of that Mystery," by those "who took a portion of the sacred Body, and abstained from the Blood of the sacred Cup[b];" how abhorrent of the "execrable"

[a] The passage is given in Routh's Scr. Opusc. ii. 139. Like Theodoret, Gelasius argues from the Eucharist to the co-existence of Natures in Christ. I may refer to my Church History, p. 379.

[b] Mansi, viii. 125, (Gelasius' ep. to Majoricus and John.) See Cave, Hist. Lit. i. 462, on these crypto-Manicheans. Compare also Leo, serm. xli. 5.

Pagan feast of the Lupercalia[c]; how unbending and imperious towards the separated Church of Constantinople[d]; how bold in proclaiming that the priesthood was essentially greater than the royalty, although in civil matters subject to it[e]. His Sacramentary is complete in three books. From it we derive, either altogether as they stand, or with more or less of alteration in their form,—(for the revisers of our offices, following the precedent set by him and by S. Gregory, took great freedom in developing the old prayers, often with very good effect,) the following Collects.

1. Morning Collect for Peace. It stands as the Post-Communion in a Gelasian Mass for Peace, Gelas., lib. iii. 56; Mur. i. 727.

"Deus auctor pacis et amator, Quem nosse vivere, Cui servire regnare est, protege ab omnibus impugnationibus supplices Tuos; ut qui defensione Tuâ fidimus, nullius hostilitatis arma timeamus. Per," &c.

In the Gregorian book it holds a similar position, Mur. ii. 203, Menard, p. 216; in the Portiforium or Breviary of Sarum it is ordered to be said "at Matins only;" the word Matins here, as of old with S. Benedict, meaning Lauds[f].

[c] Mansi, viii. 68; Robertson, Hist. Ch. i. 447.

[d] See Milman, Lat. Chr. i. 251. The quarrel was as to the memory of Acacius of Constantinople, whom Rome had denounced in 484 for communicating with Monophysites.

[e] Ep. to Anastasius. Mansi, viii. 31.

[f] Portif. Sar. fasc. ii. 175, i. 40, 89.

2. Evening Collect for Peace. A Sunday Collect, Mur. i. 690, beginning, "Omnipotens sempiterne Deus, à Quo *solo*." Also, in its usual form, the first Collect in the Mass for Peace. Mur. i. 727:—

"Deus à Quo sancta desideria et recta sunt consilia, et justa sunt opera; da servis Tuis illam quam mundus dare non potest pacem; ut et corda mandatis Tuis dedita, et hostium sublatâ formidine tempora sint Tuâ protectione tranquilla. Per," &c.

It was similarly used by S. Gregory. It was appended to the Sarum Litany, and also became the Collect of the "Memorial" for Peace, the Antiphon of which we still retain in the form of a verse and response, "Give peace in our time[g]," &c. In the Elizabethan Primer of 1559 we find a more literal rendering of it than the one which we now use. Nor can we wonder at the deep hold which it has taken through so many ages on the heart of the English Church; for surely no prayer could more impressively set forth the truth, that only in doing God's work can we enjoy His peace—that the gift which the world can neither give nor take away is for those who know Him as the Fountain of good counsels and just works.

3. Evening Collect for Aid against all Perils: among the Gelasian Vesper Collects. Mur. i. 745:—

"Illumina, quæsumus, Domine, tenebras nos-

[g] Port. Sar. i. 114, ii. 175.

tras; et totius noctis insidias repelle propitius. Per," &c.

Mr. Freeman traces it to a prayer-like hymn of the Eastern Compline, which prays for light and for deliverance from snares. It was the Compline Collect of Sarum.

4. Collect for Clergy and People. This occurs in two forms; as a Collect for a Mass in a Monastery, and as a Collect for a blessing on any particular household. Mur. i. 719, 737:—

"Omnipotens sempiterne Deus, Qui facis mirabilia magna solus; prætende super famulos Tuos (super hos famulos degentes in hac domo) Spiritum gratiæ salutaris; et ut in veritate Tibi complaceant (et ut complaceant Tibi, Deus, in veritate Tuâ) perpetuæ eis rorem Tuæ benedictionis infunde. Per," &c.

In the Gregorian it is a Collect "for an abbat or for his congregation," and they are named in it accordingly. In the English Church it became definitely a prayer for Bishops. Thus in the end of the Sarum Litany; the reading there being, "super famulos Tuos *Pontifices* et super cunctas congregationes illis commissas;"—in the Use of York it prayed, "send down on Thy servant our Archbishop," &c. "Curates" or parish priests were first named in the prayer when it was inserted in the Litany of 1544. The Latin Prayer-book of

1560 kept the reading of the Sarum Litany. The Scotch Prayer-book called it a prayer for "the holy Clergy," and named Presbyters between Bishops and Curates. Various proposals have been made[h] to alter the phrase "Who alone workest great marvels;" and in the American Prayer-book it is changed into "from Whom cometh every good and perfect gift."

5. Fourth Sunday in Advent. The second Collect "de Adventu Domini." Mur. i. 680.

6. Innocents' Day. Mur. i. 499.

7. Palm Sunday. Mur. i. 546.

8. Second Collect for Good Friday. Mur. i. 560. It is one of the solemn prayers for this day. Our third Collect is *based* upon two Gelasian ones.

9. The first half of the Collect for Easter Day. Mur. i. 573.

10. Fourth Sunday after Easter. Mur. i. 585.

11. Fifth Sunday after Easter. Mur. i. 585.

12. First Sunday after Trinity. Among the Paschal Collects. Mur. i. 587.

13. Second Sunday. Sunday after Ascension. Mur. i. 590.

14. Sixth Sunday. The first Collect in the third book of Gelasius, which contains the prayers for ordinary Sundays. Mur. i. 687.

15. Seventh Sunday. Gelas. lib. iii. 2; Mur. i. 687.

[h] Cardwell, Conferences, pp. 275, 431.

16. Eighth Sunday. Mur. i. 688.

17. The present form of the Collect for Tenth Sunday after Trinity, beginning, "Pateant aures misericordiæ." Mur. i. 689.

18. Eleventh Sunday. Mur. i. 690.

19. The present form of the Collect for Twelfth Sunday after Trinity, which is,—

"Omnipotens sempiterne Deus, Qui abundantiâ pietatis Tuæ, et merita supplicum excedis et vota: effunde super nos misericordiam Tuam; ut dimittas quæ conscientia metuit, et adjicias quod oratio non præsumit. Per[1]."

20. Fifteenth Sunday. Mur. i. 692.

21. Sixteenth Sunday. Mur. i. 692.

22. Eighteenth Sunday. Mur. i. 693.

23. Nineteenth Sunday. Mur. i. 693.

24. Twentieth Sunday. Mur. i. 694.

25. Twenty-first Sunday. Mur. i. 694.

26. "Assist us mercifully." This is the first Collect in a Mass for one about to travel; Mur. i. 703. This original purport of the prayer can only be seen by a glance at the Latin:—

"Adesto, Domine, supplicationibus nostris, et viam famuli Tui *illius* in salutis Tuæ prosperitate dispone; ut inter omnes vitæ hujus varietates Tuo semper protegatur auxilio. Per," &c.

27. The Collect of Confirmation, "Almighty

[1] Murat. i. 690.

and everliving God," which occurs in the service for Easter Eve, with this rubric prefixed to it: "Deinde ab Episcopo datur eis Spiritus septiformis; ad consignandum imponit eis manum in his verbis:"—

"Deus Omnipotens, Pater Domini nostri Jesu Christi, Qui regenerâsti famulos Tuos ex aquâ et Spiritu Sancto, Quique dedisti eis remissionem omnium peccatorum; Tu, Domine, immitte in eos Spiritum Sanctum Tuum Paraclitum, et da eis Spiritum sapientiæ et intellectûs, Spiritum consilii et fortitudinis, Spiritum scientiæ et pietatis. Adimple eos Spiritu timoris Dei, in Nomine Domini nostri Jesu Christi," &c.[k]

This prayer, as Mr. Palmer observes, "is probably much more ancient" than the time of Gelasius[l]. In Menard's Gregorian Sacramentary it begins, p. 74, "Omnipotens sempiterne Deus."

28. The prayer beginning, "O most merciful God," in the Visitation Office. This appears as the "Reconciliatio pœnitentis ad mortem," Mur. i. 552.

29. The first collect in the Commination, "O Lord, we beseech Thee." This is the first prayer said over penitents, Mur. i. 504.

[k] Mur. i. 571.

[l] Orig. Lit. ii. 203. Had Dean Alford been aware of the history of our Confirmation Collect, he could hardly have referred to it, in his notes on Acts viii., as *not* affirming any bestowal of the Holy Spirit in Confirmation, but only "recognizing the former reception of the Spirit at Baptism, and praying for an increase of His influence." It plainly affirms a special gift.

These are the Collects which have been derived to us *originally* from this venerable Service-book: to which may also be traced the substance of some portions of the long Collect before the imposition of hands in the Consecration of Bishops, not to speak of a few words which, as belonging to the Canon of the Mass, are much older than the Sacramentary which contains them. These words are, "may be fulfilled with Thy grace and heavenly benediction," "not weighing our merits, but pardoning our offences," "by Whom and with Whom," &c. "Omni benedictione cœlesti et gratiâ repleamur;—non æstimator meriti, sed veniæ, quæsumus, largitor.—Per Ipsum et cum Ipso...est Tibi Deo Patri Omnipotenti in unitate Sp. Sancti omnis honor et gloria," &c.

About a hundred years after Gelasius, Gregory the Great sat on the throne of Rome, A.D. 590—604. His Sacramentary, so deeply reverenced and widely adopted in the West, and often bound in gold, silver, and ivory, was compiled on the principle of condensing and shortening the Gelasian work. The biographer of Gregory, John the Deacon, in the second chapter of the second book of his Life, says that he withdrew many things from the Gelasian books, altered a few, and added some, and made one book instead of three. One instance of abbreviation was in the reduction of the Collects at Mass from five or six to three only[m]; and it is also believed that he introduced a change into the practice as to Prefaces—fixing a small number instead of a great variety. This Sacramentary has been edited by Pamelius, Rocca, Hugh Menard, (whom the Benedictines follow,) and Muratori. A perfectly pure text cannot, Muratori thinks, be hoped for; he prefers Pamelius' text to Menard's; but he adopts, in his edition, the Vatican manuscript, instead of that of the monastery of S. Eligius, which had been followed by Menard and the Benedictines. In the Sacramentary, as he has edited it, we find the *original sources* of the following Collects.

1. S. Stephen. Mur. ii. 12; see Menard, p. 8.
2. S. John Evangelist. Mur. ii. 13; Men. p. 9.
3. Epiphany. Mur. ii. 16; Men. p. 15. Our English version hardly exhibits the full antithesis between *fides* and *species*, 2 Cor. v. 7.
4. First Sunday after Epiphany. Mur. ii. 159. "Dominica prima post Theophania." See also Mur. ii. 16; Men. p. 17.
5. Second Sunday. Mur. ii. 159; Men. p. 18.
6. Third Sunday. Mur. ii. 160; Men. p. 25.
7. Fourth Sunday. Mur. ii. 160; Men. p. 26.
8. Fifth Sunday. Mur. ii. 161; Men. p. 26.
9. Septuagesima. Mur. ii. 26; Men. p. 32.

[m] Mabillon, de Lit. Gall. i. 2. 4.

10. Sexagesima. Mur. ii. 27; Men. p. 32. This Collect in its original form spoke of "the protection of the Doctor of the Gentiles."

11. Second Sunday in Lent. Mur. ii. 35; Men. p. 42.

12. Third Sunday. Mur. ii. 39; Men. p. 46.

13. Fourth Sunday. Mur. ii. 43; Men. p. 50.

14. Fifth Sunday. Mur. ii. 47; Men. p. 55.

15. First Collect for Good Friday. A final prayer "super populum" on Wednesday before Easter, Mur. ii. 54; Men. p. 64.

16. The second half of the Easter Day Collect. Mur. ii. 67; Men. p. 75. The words which Gregory substituted for the Gelasian are striking as a terse and vigorous summary of the doctrine of grace:—"Vota nostra, quæ præveniendo adspiras, etiam adjuvando prosequere."

17. Ascension Day. Mur. ii. 85; Men. p. 95.

18. Whitsunday. Mur. ii. 90; Men. p. 98.

19. Third Sunday after Trinity. Mur. ii. 165; Men. p. 177[a].

20. Fourth Sunday. Mur. ii. 166; Men. p. 178.

21. Seventeenth Sunday after Trinity. Mur. ii. 172; Men. p. 188. Another Collect on preventing grace.

22. Twenty-second Sunday. Mur. ii. 175. Not in Menard.

[a] The Sundays of this series are called "after Trinity" in Sarum.

23. Twenty-third Sunday. Mur. ii. 175; Men. p. 194.

24. Twenty-fourth Sunday. This is a Sunday Collect for "the seventh month," Mur. ii. 121; in Men. p. 188, 18th week after Pentecost [o].

25. Twenty-fifth Sunday. Mur. ii. 176; Men. p. 195. The word "Excita," with which this Collect begins, had been used in the Gelasian Advent Collects in connection both with man's "heart" and God's "power."

26. Purification. Collect for the "Hypapante," (the Greek name for this feast of the "meeting" between the Holy Family and Symeon,) Mur. ii. 23. This name is not given in Men. p. 23.

27. Annunciation. A final prayer for this day's Mass, Mur. ii. 26; in Men. p. 31, a *super oblata.*

28. S. Michael and all Angels. For the "Dedicatio Basilicæ Sancti Angeli." Mur. ii. 125; Men. p. 135.

29. The first part of "We humbly beseech Thee, O Father." In the original, "Sanctorum Tuorum intercessione averte." Mur. ii. 119.

30. The beautiful Collect, "O God, Whose nature." The last prayer in a Mass for sins, Mur. ii. 200; in Men. p. 204, a "collect for sins." Part of it is almost copied from the Gelasian in Mur. i. 551, "ut quos delictorum catena constringit

[o] The arrangement of Collects for this season is not quite the same in Menard and in Muratori.

magnitudo Tuæ pietatis absolvat." It was at the end of the *preces* in the Sarum Litany, and also appeared in the Litany of 1544. Under Edward VI. it was not used, but it re-appeared in the Book of 1559. The criticism passed upon this prayer by the Commissioners of 1689 is worth remembering for its stupidity: "full of strange and impertinent expressions, and, besides, not in the original, but foisted in since by another hand[p]."

31. "Prevent us, O Lord." For Ember Saturday in Lent, Mur. ii. 34; Men. p. 41. It may be compared with the Easter Collect:—

"Actiones nostras, quæsumus, Domine, et adspirando præveni, et adjuvando prosequere; ut cuncta nostra operatio à Te semper incipiat, et per Te cœpta finiatur. Per," &c.

It became a favourite Collect for use before and after the Celebration: thus in the rites of York and Hereford it was said before the "Confiteor[q]."

32. "Almighty and immortal God," in the Baptismal Office. This prayer is appointed to be said over a male catechumen in the Gregorian rites of Holy Saturday, Mur. ii. 155. It thus came into the Sarum Order for Making a Catechumen, Maskell, p. 7.

[p] Cardwell, Conferences, p. 431. The Collect may in truth remind us of that sweet compassion which grieved for the fair-faced Yorkshire boys who were "in bondage to the prince of darkness," Bede, ii. 1.

[q] Martene, i. 675, 6. Maskell, Anc. Lit., p. 8.

33. The first sentence of the first Collect at Burial is substantially Gregorian, Mur. ii. 216[r].

There are several other Collects which appear in Menard's edition, but are excluded, or placed in an appendix, by Muratori. A short form of our Third Morning Collect, the germs of which we have already seen in a Gelasian one, ("We give Thee thanks, holy Lord," &c.) is inserted by Menard on the authority of one MS.:—

"Deus, Qui nos ad principium hujus diei pervenire fecisti, da nobis hunc diem sine peccato transire; ut in nullo à Tuis semitis declinemus, sed ad Tuam justitiam faciendam nostra semper procedant eloquia. Per," &c. Men. p. 212.

The Collect came into general use at the Office of Prime; but it assumed different forms in the Roman and English offices.

Roman.	*English.*
Lord God Almighty, Who hast made us to come to the beginning of this day, save us this day by Thy power; that in this day we turn aside into no sin, but that our words may go forth, our	Holy Lord, Father Almighty, eternal God, Who hast made us to come to the beginning of this day, save us this day by Thy power, and grant that this day we turn aside into no sin,

[r] The word "faithful" was substituted in 1661 for "elected," which was true to the original, "in Quo *electorum* animæ, deposito carnis onere, plenâ felicitate lætantur."

thoughts and deeds be directed, to do always what is righteous in Thy sight. (Domin. ad Prim.)

nor run into any danger; but that all our doings may be ordered by Thy governance, to do always what is righteous in Thy sight. (Ad Prim.)

Our glorious Collect for Trinity Sunday is given by Menard for the Octave of Pentecost; Muratori exhibits it as part of "an addition to the Othobon Codex." The present English version, unfortunately, somewhat obscures the thought of the original, "ut ejusdem Fidei firmitate ab omnibus semper muniamur adversis," i.e. that *by* stedfastness in this Faith we are to be safe from evil,—that our Creed is to be the shield of our life. This grand thought was manifest in the Collect until the revision of 1661 [a].

The "Collect for Purity," as we commonly call it, is similarly placed by Muratori, ii. 383, as belonging to a Mass of the Holy Spirit. It begins, "Deus Cui omne cor patet, et omnis voluntas loquitur." In the Sarum Ordinary of the Mass, it was the first Collect said by the priest, before the "Introibo ad altare." This explains the position which it has held in our reformed Liturgy since 1549. It was also said at the end of the York Litany.

[a] For several old versions, see Maskell, Mon. Rit. ii. 28.

The Collect for S. Paul's Conversion is developed from one given by Menard, p. 22. Another, similar to it in the first sentence, is given by Muratori for the "Natale S. Pauli" on June 30. The Collect for S. Bartholomew is derived, as to its second part, from one which appears in Menard, p. 125. The Collect, "O Almighty Lord and everlasting God," is not quite identical with one given by Menard, p. 213, but occurs at the end of the Sarum Prime, in a shorter form than that now exhibited in the Roman Breviary.

It was natural that England should receive the Gregorian Sacramentary sooner than "any other country beyond the Roman patriarchate[t];" for it was the Communion-book of him whom the best of the Anglo-Saxons, as Bede and Archbishop Egbert of York[u], were wont to call their master and apostle; who was formally styled "our Father," clearly in an emphatic sense, by that Council of Cloveshoo, in 747, which alludes to the ritual of the Church of Rome[x]. Mr. Freeman thinks that S. Augustine of Canterbury, acting on S. Gregory's wise advice,—to adopt any good elements of ritual which he could find in various Churches[y],—brought into England the Gallican Daily Office; but he adds that, at the same time, he introduced the Roman Communion

[t] Palmer, Orig. Lit. i. 124. [u] Bede, ii. 1; Egbert's Answers, No. 16. 1.
[x] Johnson's English Canons, i. 250. [y] Bede, i. 27.

Office [z]; and this fact is undoubted, although it is very probable, as Lingard says, that he borrowed from the French Eucharistic rite the custom of a solemn episcopal benediction, divided into three or more sentences, given just after the breaking of the Blessed Sacrament. This custom was not practised by Gregory the Great [a], though many such benedictions were circulated under his name; and part of one of these appears to have suggested our Circumcision Collect.

Some other parts of our present Liturgy are taken from Collects which the Church of England used in the Middle Ages, but which are not found in the Gregorian or preceding Sacramentaries. I may adduce the prayer in the Litany, "O God, merciful Father," which belonged to the Sarum Mass "for tribulation of heart [b]," and is also found in the Missal published by Illyricus; several parts of the prayers of Matrimony, as, "O God of Abraham," &c., and portions also of two Visitation Collects.

The ancient Collects which we still use might be divided into two classes:—

1. Those in which there has been *no real alteration*, but only, at the most, the *addition* of words

[z] Principles of Divine Service, i. 253.
[a] See Lingard, Ang.-S. Ch. i. 295; Murat. i. 81; Pont. Egb., p. vii.
[b] "Part of the rich deposit of the Church of Sarum." Bishop Forbes on the Litany, p. 244.

which may be said to be implied in the original, as "good, great, holy, hearty, mighty, true, only, evil, grace, help, tender love, graciously, continually;" the *omission* of like words, as "kindness, heavenly;" or the *substitution* of one equivalent phrase for another, as of "true" for "worthy," or "cheerfully" for "with free minds;" the sense, in these cases, remaining as it was. To this class belong the Third Morning and Second Evening Collect, and those for Epiphany, First and Second Sundays after Epiphany, Septuagesima, Third, Fourth, Fifth and Sixth in Lent; Good Friday, first and second; Easter-day, Third and Fifth after Easter; Ascension Day; Whit-Sunday; Trinity, First, Third, Fifth, Tenth, Fourteenth, Fifteenth, Sixteenth, Seventeenth, Twentieth, Twenty-first, Twenty-third, Twenty-fourth after Trinity; Purification, Annunciation, S. Michael; and perhaps two or three more.

2. Those in which a *real alteration* has taken place; either by important *addition*, as of the words, "Who art always more ready to hear than we to pray;" "race set before us;" "light of Thy truth;" "hast ordained strength," &c.; "assault and hurt the soul;" "keep us, we beseech Thee," &c.; "the way of Thy commandments;" "may so faithfully serve Thee;" "may show forth our thankfulness;" and the larger part of the Col-

lect for S. Stephen; with some other passages. Or by important *omission*, as of (loving Thee) "*in* all things." Or by important *substitution*, as of "Whose service is perfect freedom" for "Whom to serve is to reign;" "perils and dangers" for "snares;" "in Thy true religion" or "in continual godliness," for "with continual kindness;" "as may support us in all dangers," &c., for "that by Thy help we may overcome the things which we suffer for our sins;" "Who alone canst order the unruly wills and affections of sinful men," for "Who makest the minds of faithful men to be of one will[b];" "through things temporal," for "through temporal good," &c.; "nourish us with all goodness," for "nourish what is good;" "who cannot do anything that is good without Thee," for "who cannot exist without Thee;" "temptations of the world, the flesh, and the devil," for "infections of the devil;" "Thy Holy Spirit," for "Thy merciful working;" "Who didst give to Thine Apostle Bartholomew grace," &c., for "Who hast given us the venerable and holy joy of this day in the festival of the blessed Bartholomew," &c. Other changes might be named; two have been referred to already, as substituting a reference to God's glory and protection for the patronage and protection of

[b] A change which, like many others, dates from 1661.

Saints. Among the many collects which belong to this class, may be named the Second Morning Collect, the Third for Evening, and those for Fourth in Advent, S. John the Evangelist, Innocents, Fifth after Epiphany, Sexagesima, Second in Lent, Fourth after Trinity, Second, Sixth, Ninth, Eleventh, Twelfth, Thirteenth, Eighteenth, Nineteenth, Twenty-second after Trinity, Conversion of S. Paul, S. Bartholomew.

One other point in regard to this goodly heritage of our fathers may be mentioned—the influence which it has exerted over those who have been employed to make new Collects. These Collects are new, and yet not new; they may be less concise and nervous than the work of Gelasius or of Gregory, but they are instinct with the same spirit, and seem likely to exhibit the same imperishable freshness and vitality. The men who could frame our Collects for Christmas Day and Easter Even, for the Sixth Sunday after Epiphany and for All Saints, had profited well by their familiarity with the majestic forms which they were called upon to imitate. It was but natural for them to retain the ecclesiastical language, for they knew how to value and hold fast the precious gift of ecclesiastical continuity. Their compositions may be thus arranged in order of time:—

1. In 1549; First and Second in Advent, Christ-

mas Day, Circumcision, Quinquagesima, Ash Wednesday, First in Lent, Third for Good Friday, First and Second after Easter, and those Saint's-day Collects which have not been already referred to Latin originals, excepting S. Andrew; the present form of "We humbly beseech Thee;" the two Communion Collects for the King; the Collect of Humble Access; the present second Post-Communion prayer [c]; the third, fifth, and sixth of the six Collects appended to the Communion Office; the Collects for Rain and Fair Weather; the original form of the second Ember Collect; the first Baptismal Collect [d]; the original form of the prayer for sanctification of the water; the second Confirmation Collect (which Mr. Palmer, without sufficient reason, identifies with a prayer of Archbishop Egbert [e];) portions of Visitation Collects; the Communion Collect of the Sick; the Burial Collect properly so called, (appointed, in 1549, for a Celebration at Burials); the Churching Collect; the second Commination Collect; the Collects of the Ordinal.

2. In 1552; S. Andrew, the two Collects in time

[c] In both these, as in other Collects of 1549, some changes have been made since.

[d] The second, as we have seen, is Gregorian; the third, "Almighty and everlasting God, heavenly Father," was adopted in 1549 from the ritual of Herman Archbishop of Cologne.

[e] Orig. Lit. ii. 205. Much as our Liturgical literature owes to Mr. Palmer, it is to be regretted that he indulges, not unfrequently, in unreal parallels between the old and the new.

of Dearth, Collect in time of War, in time of Plague; the Baptismal Thanksgiving, "We yield Thee hearty thanks[f];" the present form (on the whole) of the first prayer at Burial.

3. In 1559; the prayer for the Queen's Majesty, which had already appeared in authorized books of devotion.

4. In 1604; the Collect for the Royal Family, the Thanksgivings for Rain, Fair Weather, Deliverance from Enemies, Deliverance from Plague.

5. In 1661; Third Sunday in Advent; the main part of Collect for S. Stephen; Sixth Sunday after Epiphany, Easter Even, (based on one in the Scotch Prayer-book of 1636,) first Ember Collect, Prayer for Parliament, (previously in occasional forms of Prayer, 1625 and 1628,) Prayer for all Conditions, General Thanksgiving, Thanksgiving for restoring Public Peace, Prayers for a sick child, for a sick person not likely to recover, the Commendatory Prayer, and that for persons troubled in mind, with those for use at Sea; and parts of other Collects.

It only remains to classify our Liturgical Collects according to the various spiritual needs of

[f] We generally associate the revision of 1552 with such changes as it wrought in our Sacramental services. It is well to remember that, if it took away much, it gave us a new and emphatic assertion of the regeneration of baptized infants, and seven additional repetitions of the Athanasian Creed.

Christian people, so as to assist those who desire to incorporate them into private or family prayer.

1. *For the Spirit of acceptable Prayer.* Third and Tenth after Trinity.

2. *For Repentance.* Ash Wednesday, S. John Baptist.

3. *For Pardon.* "O God, Whose nature," Septuagesima, Fourth in Lent, Twelfth, Twenty-first, Twenty-fourth after Trinity, First in Commination.

4. *For Faith.* Trinity Sunday, S. Thomas, S. Mark. The Annunciation Collect may be used as a daily memorial of the mystery of the Incarnation.

5. *For Hope of Heavenly Blessedness.* Second in Advent, S. Stephen, Fourth after Easter.

6. *For Love.* Quinquagesima, Second, Sixth, Seventh after Trinity.

7. *For Faith, Hope, and Love.* Fourteenth after Trinity.

8. *For Purity.* Innocents, Circumcision, Sixth after Epiphany, First in Lent, Easter Even, First after Easter, Eighteenth after Trinity, Purification, "Almighty God, unto Whom."

9. *For Unworldliness.* Fourth after Easter, Ascension, S. John Baptist, S. James, S. Matthew.

10. *For Devotion of Will to God.* Second Evening Collect, Twentieth and Twenty-fifth after Trinity, S. Andrew.

11. *For Renewal.* Christmas Day.

12. *For Illumination.* **S. John the Evangelist.**

13. *For Right Intentions.* **Fifth after Easter, Ninth after Trinity.**

14. *For the carrying-out of such Intentions.* **Easter Day, "Prevent us."**

15. *For Grace to know God's will.* **First after Epiphany, Whitsunday.**

16. *For Grace to do His Will.* **First and Fourth in Advent, First, Eleventh, Thirteenth, Seventeenth, Twentieth, Twenty-fifth after Trinity, SS. Philip and James.**

17. *For Grace to use His Gifts.* **S. Barnabas.**

18. *For Grace to love His Word.* **Second Sunday in Advent, S. Paul, S. Luke, S. Bartholomew.**

19. *For Defence against Danger, or Deliverance from Evil.* **Second and Third Morning Collects, Third, Fourth, Fifth after Epiphany, Sexagesima, Second, Third, and Fifth in Lent, Second, Third, Eighth, Fifteenth, Sixteenth, Twentieth, Twenty-second after Trinity, S. Michael.**

20. *For Comfort.* **Sunday after Ascension, Whitsunday.**

21. *For Guidance.* **Fourth and Nineteenth after Trinity; "Assist us;" "O Almighty Lord."**

22. *For the Benefit of Christ's Example.* **Palm Sunday, Second after Easter.**

23. *For the Benefit of Christ's Sacrifice.* **Second after Easter, Annunciation.**

24. *For Conformity to the Christian Standard.* Third after Easter, All Saints.

25. *For Peace.* Second Morning and Evening Collects, Second after Epiphany, Fifth after Trinity.

26. *For the Church and its Work.* Collect for Clergy and People, S. John, Fifth after Epiphany, Good Friday, Fifth, Fifteenth, Sixteenth, Twenty-second after Trinity, S. Matthias, S. Peter, S. Bartholomew, SS. Simon and Jude.

27. *For Final Blessedness.* Epiphany, Sixth and Thirteenth after Trinity.

28. *At the Close of Prayers.* Twelfth and Twenty-third after Trinity; "Assist us;" "Almighty God, the fountain of all wisdom;" "Almighty God, Who hast promised to hear."

I venture to place here, by themselves, a few Collects constructed in imitation of the ancient model.

For the Spirit of Prayer. O Almighty God, from Whom every good prayer cometh, and Who pourest out on all who desire it the Spirit of grace and supplications; deliver us, when we draw nigh to Thee, from coldness of heart and wanderings of mind; that with stedfast thoughts and kindled affections we may worship Thee in spirit and in truth; through Jesus Christ our Lord.

Sunday Morning. O God, Who makest us glad

with the weekly remembrance of the glorious Resurrection of Thy Son our Lord; vouchsafe us this day such a blessing through Thy worship, that the days which follow it may be spent in Thy favour; through the same Jesus Christ our Lord.

Sunday Evening. O Lord, Who by triumphing over the powers of darkness, didst prepare our place in the New Jerusalem; grant us, who have this day given thanks for Thy Resurrection, to praise Thee in that City whereof Thou art the Light; where with the Father, &c.

Before Study of Scripture. O Lord Jesus Christ, Who art the Truth Incarnate and the Teacher of the faithful; let Thy Spirit overshadow us in reading Thy Word, and conform our thoughts to Thy Revelation; that learning of Thee with honest hearts, we may be rooted and built up in Thee, Who livest, &c.

For Guidance. O God, by Whom the meek are guided in judgment, and light riseth up in darkness for the godly; grant us, in all our doubts and uncertainties, the grace to ask what Thou wouldest have us to do; that the Spirit of wisdom may save us from all false choices, and that in Thy light we may see light, and in Thy straight path may not stumble; through Jesus Christ our Lord.

For Cheerfulness. O most loving Father, Who

willest us to give thanks for all things, to dread nothing but the loss of Thee, and to cast all our care on Thee Who carest for us; preserve us from faithless fears and worldly anxieties, and grant that no clouds of this mortal life may hide from us the light of that Love which is immortal, and which Thou hast manifested unto us in Thy Son, Jesus Christ our Lord.

For Grace to speak the Truth in Love. O Lord and Saviour Christ, Who camest not to strive nor cry, but to let Thy words fall as the drops that water the earth; grant all who contend for the Faith once delivered, never to injure it by clamour and impatience; but speaking Thy precious Truth in love, so to present it that it may be loved, and that men may see in it Thy goodness and Thy beauty; Who livest, &c.

Against Spiritual Apathy. O God, the Sovereign Good of the soul, Who requirest the hearts of all Thy children; deliver us from all sloth in Thy work, all coldness in Thy cause; and grant us by looking unto Thee to rekindle our love, and by waiting upon Thee to renew our strength; through Jesus Christ our Lord.

For Hatred of Sin. O God, Whom none can love except they hate the thing that is evil, and Who willedst by Thy Son our Saviour to redeem us from all iniquity; deliver us when we are tempted to look on sin without abhorrence, and let the virtue of His Passion come between us and the enemy of our souls; through the same Jesus Christ our Lord.

On the Incarnation. We adore Thee, Blessed Jesus, very God and very Man, the Same yesterday, and to-day, and for ever, our strong Salvation and our only Hope. Take us, we pray Thee, into Thy keeping, both now and at the hour of our death; make us faithful to Thee upon earth, and blessed with Thee in Heaven, where with the Father, &c.

On the Example of the Blessed Virgin. O Christ our God Incarnate, Whose Virgin Mother was blessed in bearing Thee, but still more blessed in keeping Thy word; grant us, who honour the exaltation of her lowliness, to follow the example of her devotion to Thy will, Who livest, &c.

On the Communion of Saints. O God, Who hast brought us near to an innumerable company of Angels, and to the spirits of just men made perfect; grant us during our pilgrimage to abide in their fellowship, and in our Country to become partakers of their joy; through Jesus Christ our Lord.

For a Friend. I pray Thee, good Lord Jesus, by the love which Thou hadst for him that lay on Thy bosom, to make me thankful for all that Thou hast given me in Thy servant *N.* and to bless *him* exceeding abundantly, above all that I can ask or think. Help us to love each other in Thee and for Thee, to be one in heart through all separations, and to walk as friends in the path of Thy service; and finally unite us for ever at Thy feet, where peace and love are perfect and immortal, and Thou, with the Father, &c.

For the Clergy. Bless, we beseech Thee, O Lord, Thy whole Clergy, that they may handle Thy holy things with holiness, and be pleasing to Thee Who art our Priest for ever.

For all who do the Work of the Church. O Lord, without Whom our labour is but lost, and with Whom Thy little ones go forth as the mighty; be present to all works in Thy Church which are undertaken according to Thy will, (especially in *N. N.*,) and grant to Thy labourers a pure intention, patient faith, sufficient success upon earth, and the bliss of serving Thee in Heaven; through Jesus Christ our Lord.

For Sufferers. Lord Jesus Christ, our sympathizing Saviour, Who for man didst bear the Agony and the Cross; draw Thou near to Thy suffering servants, in their pain of body or trouble of mind, (especially *N. N.*;) hallow all their crosses in this life, and crown them hereafter where all tears are wiped away; where with the Father, &c.

For the Tempted. Merciful and faithful High

Priest, Who didst deign for us to be tempted of Satan; make speed to aid Thy servants who are assaulted by manifold temptations; and as Thou knowest their several infirmities, let each one find Thee mighty to save, Who livest, &c.

For those who live in Sin. Have mercy, O compassionate Father, on all who are hardened through the deceitfulness of sin; vouchsafe them grace to come to themselves, the will and power to return to Thee, and the loving welcome of Thy forgiveness; through Jesus Christ our Lord.

For those who err from the Faith. Almighty and everliving God, Who hast given us the Catholic Faith of Christ for a light to our feet amid the darkness of this world; have pity upon all who, by doubting or denying it, are gone astray from the path of safety; bring home the Truth to their hearts, and grant them to receive it as little children; through the same Jesus Christ our Lord.

THE END.

Printed by Messrs. Parker, Cornmarket, Oxford.

7
35

Ingram Content Group UK Ltd.
Milton Keynes UK
UKHW021959150623
423530UK00005B/120

9 781015 934825